Laurel

Laurel

Modern American Flavors in Philadelphia

Nicholas Elmi and Adam Erace

RUNNING PRESS
PHILADELPHIA

Running Press
Hachette Book Group
1290 Avenue of the Americas, New York, NY 10104
www.runningpress.com
@Running_Press

Printed in China

First Edition: September 2019

Published by Running Press, an imprint of Perseus Books, LLC, a subsidiary of Hachette Book Group, Inc.
The Running Press name and logo is a trademark of the Hachette Book Group.

The Hachette Speakers Bureau provides a wide range of authors for speaking events.
To find out more, go to www.hachettespeakersbureau.com or call (866) 376-6591.

The publisher is not responsible for websites (or their content) that are not owned by the publisher.

Print book cover and interior design by Joshua McDonnell

Library of Congress Control Number: 2018961686

ISBNs: 978-0-7624-9173-5 (hardcover), 978-0-7624-9172-8 (ebook)

1010

10   9   8   7   6   5   4   3   2   1

For my beautiful wife and children

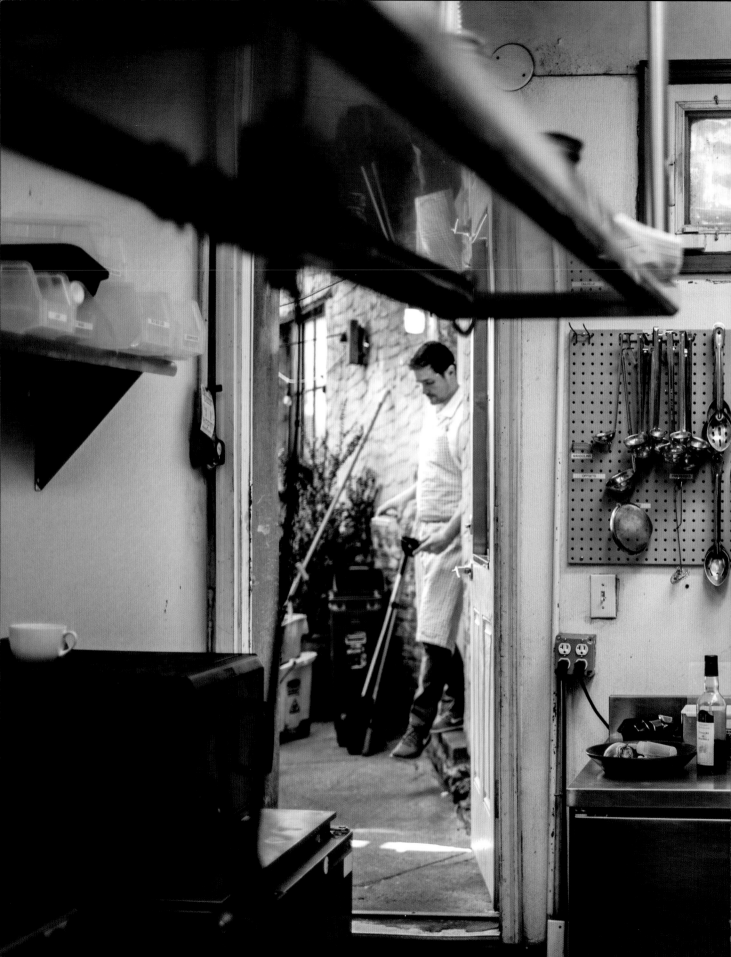

FALL

WINTER

Frozen Beet, Sumac, Pomegranate

Kasu-Cured Fluke, Citrus, Olive Oil

Warm Truffle Custard, Surf Clam, Makrut Lime

Pan-Roasted Halibut Cheek,
White Asparagus, Quince Confit

Bourbon-Glazed Grilled Lobster,
Crunchy Grains, Apple Blossoms

Fresh Ricotta Gnocchi, Black Truffle, Toasted Sourdough

Black Trumpet Mushroom–Stuffed Dover Sole,
Chicken Jus, Whey Onions

Hay-Cured Squab en Vessie

Yuzu Curd, Black Sesame, Torched Malt Crisp

Cocktail: The Kali

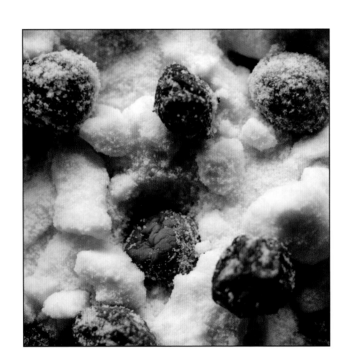

SPRING

Daylily Shoots, Dried Beef Heart

Cardamom Leaf–Cured Bream,
Young and Old Peaches

Wellfleet Oyster Cream, Pinelands Roots, Sochan

Steamed Pennsylvania Bamboo,
Egg, Chicken, Green Polenta

Shaved Asparagus, Frog Leg Confit,
Wild Nettles, Jalapeño

Grilled Shrimp, Spring Ferments

Black Sea Bass, Peas, Rhubarb

Braised Lamb Neck, Green Garlic, Ground Ivy Jus

Honeysuckle-Poached Rhubarb, Ice Cream,
Knotweed Jam, Lovage Granite

Cocktail: A Bird Named Barb

SUMMER

INTRODUCTION

FIVE THOUSAND CASH AND TEQUILA

We opened Laurel, a modern American restaurant steeped in French tradition, in a tiny space on East Passyunk Avenue in South Philly in 2013. I had just finished filming *Top Chef,* but it was before the finale aired. I knew I had won, but I couldn't tell anyone besides my wife, Kristen. There were confidentiality agreements; everything was top secret.

I had quit my last chef job, at Rittenhouse Tavern in Center City, to do the show. Before that I worked for Georges Perrier for thirteen years on and off, first at Brasserie Perrier, then at Le Bec-Fin, where I was the head chef for three and a half years. I knew it was time to open my own place. We had been looking and looking for a space all around the city. Lee Styer had been my sous chef at Le Bec for six months and left in 2008 to open Fond on Passyunk. He had moved the restaurant to a larger location across from the Singing Fountain, which is like the town square of our neighborhood, with a fountain in the center that plays music. When it's warm out, little kids splash around in the water. There's a small farmers' market on Wednesdays. At Christmas, the neighborhood association puts up a big tree and has a lighting ceremony with hot cider and carols.

I have a special attachment to East Passyunk. When I first moved to Philly in 2000 to work at Brasserie Perrier, I crashed on my brother's couch for a month, then moved to an apartment with my sous chef at the time and his wife on 13th and Morris Streets, a couple of blocks off "the Avenue," as locals call it. There was no fountain then, no farmers' market, none of the restaurants that would eventually come to define Passyunk as one of the city's best dining strips. But I liked it here. It was clean and safe and felt like a real neighborhood. This is the first place I lived, in what was to me a new city. I grew up in West Newbury, Massachusetts, on the Merrimack River. I came to Philly to cook and never left.

By the time I was ready to open Laurel and looking for a space, the Avenue was gaining traction. There were great restaurants like Paradiso and Will and cool small shops. *Food & Wine* named East Passyunk one of the top food destinations in America. There was a real energy down here that I wanted to be a part of. What I loved about the area so much, and still love about it, is that all the successful restaurants have chefs that are *in* their restaurants. People who open restaurants here are people who want to be in the kitchen, who want to have their hands in the food. That creates a realness to the cuisine and the restaurants.

So Lee's original space was sitting empty. He was thinking of doing a brunch place or a gallery, but while we were playing poker at his house one night, we drank tequila and I persuaded him to sublease it to me. I gave him $5,000 cash, and he said I could have the lease. Four months later, Laurel was open.

A COMFORTABLE PLACE

I was twenty-seven when I started working at Le Bec-Fin, and after three and half years there, I was a mess. I don't know how my wife stayed with me. During my first year there we went through thirty-two cooks. *Thirty-two.*

For a cook in Philly at that time, Le Bec was the peak of the professional mountain. It had been considered the best restaurant in the city for forty years, a temple of French fine dining that had put Philly on the culinary map in 1970. (Chef Perrier has a street named after him, to give you an idea of his notoriety.) The environment was very intense. Chef thrives in chaos. He needed to yell, he needed to scream, something had to be wrong all the time. We would make the porcini sauce for our ravioli, for example. I'd take a quart upstairs for service, and he would say, "It's perfect!" The next day, I would bring him a quart of the *very same* batch of sauce to taste, and he would say, "It's shit!" It messes with your head, to the point where I was almost broken by the time I left.

But he was also very paternal. When I'm with him—and we have a great relationship now—I treat him as if he's my father. When my old chefs ask about him, they say, "How's Father?" When things were bad at Le Bec, we wouldn't talk about quitting. We talked about running away.

I never got the chance. In 2012, Chef sold Le Bec. The new owner called the entire staff into the dining room, along with the new chef, and said that everyone had the opportunity to keep their job. I spoke up, "Except for me, right?" To go through almost four years at Le Bec and have it capped by that. . . . I left with a chip on my shoulder.

When I opened Laurel, I didn't know exactly what I wanted it to be, but I knew I didn't want it to be Le Bec. During the entire time I had been the chef at Le Bec, not one of my friends came in to eat. But I understood. Nobody wants to sit down in a stuffy dining room. Nobody wants to be uncomfortable in a restaurant, physically or emotionally.

A quick story: my wife and I went with two other couples to a very famous restaurant two years ago, and the service . . . well, they weren't very nice to us. It was like they looked down on us because we *only* ordered three bottles of wine instead of six or ten. We were shoulder to shoulder at a four top—six people at a table meant for four—and we spent $1,400 per couple. I don't like that feeling. And I didn't like what we did at Le Bec either. We had regulars that came in every week and spent thousands of dollars on wine. It was like we knew whom we were going to make money off of, and if we didn't think we were going to make money off of you, we were going to get you in and get you out quickly. It was cold and detached.

Every day at Laurel, I try to remember those feelings and make sure we don't treat people that way. I want it to be a comfortable place. We have less than five hundred square feet to work with in the dining room, but the chairs are big and comfortable and the tables are large. Sometimes I have to tell my staff to chill out, take a deep breath, and smile. People come to Laurel—to any restaurant—to have a good time. If you're not having fun as a server, then the diners aren't going to have fun. If you're stiff or too ceremonial, they're going to feel like they're in a formal restaurant. And that's not what we are.

THE TASTING MENU

Because I didn't want to be associated with the formality of a tasting menu, we opened Laurel as an à la carte restaurant. But within the first couple of months, we noticed that although some customers ordered every single dish on the menu, others might split an appetizer, each get an entrée, share a dessert, and bounce. You can do that with an à la carte menu. Going out to eat can be an expensive proposition, and many people save up to do it. We wanted to be conscious of that, while also giving diners the full expression of what we do in the kitchen, of our style of food. We transitioned to a tasting-menu-only restaurant a year and a half after we opened. We now offer six- and nine-course options.

There's been a lot of debate lately between chefs, diners, and food journalists about the merits of tasting menus. The main argument from the anti-tasting camp is that tasting menus give all the control to the chef and minimize the agency of the diner, who is subject to the will of a capricious artist. I get that. But I don't think of myself that way. Sure, I make food that I hope my customers will see as beautiful, but the chef-as-*artiste* thing just doesn't feel true to me. I think chefs are more like masons or carpenters. Cooking is physical work, and although creativity is critical in a kitchen, so is consistency.

When you sit down to dinner at Laurel, we don't give you a menu. We ask if there's anything you can't eat or don't eat, and we go from there. We want it to be like you're going to somebody's house. If you invited me over to dinner at your house, I wouldn't sit down at your dining room table and say, "I'll have the fish." I'd eat whatever you made me.

When building each day's tasting menu, we think about flow: if we're going to do something that's a savory umami bomb, like our Burgundy snail dish (page 24), what do we do for the next course to lighten it up and bring you back? Because you can't serve a heavy, salty dish back to back with another heavy, salty dish. Everything has a place. That basic principle formulates our opinion on what we're doing and where we're putting stuff on the menu. We want to give you a thoughtful progression of temperatures, textures, and flavors.

It takes a really long time for us to get a dish on the menu: about two to three weeks and ten iterations before a dish ever sees the dining room. Central to the creation of a new dish are four questions:

1. What ingredient are we working with that might feel unfamiliar to our guests?

2. What technique are we using to showcase it or highlight it, to make it more intense, whether through concentrating or fermenting, or to mellow it out?

3. What ingredient are we using in an unexpected way—for example, a savory ingredient you wouldn't think of in a pastry dish, or a sweet ingredient you wouldn't think of in a savory one?

4. How will it look? What is the surprise, the wow factor? If I'm dropping a dish in front of you, what's going to make you think, "This is awesome, this is beautiful, and I can't wait to eat it."

Our approach is to find the best product and treat it with as much respect as possible. In Philadelphia, we are surrounded by some of the most fertile farmland in the country, and we work with Pennsylvania and New Jersey farmers like the Brendle family of Green Meadow Farm, Ben Wenk of Three Springs Fruit Farm, Alex Wenger of Field's Edge Research Farm, Evan Strusinski, David Siller, and Diane Gabler of Pinelands Produce to source amazing product all through the year.

Laurel is often tagged as a French restaurant because of my background, but although we use lots of French technique, we're an American restaurant. Ninety-nine percent of the product is American. But we also do Italian things. We do Japanese things. We do French things. And that's what it means to be an American restaurant right now. In this industry, there's an impulse to label and categorize, both the type of food you're cooking and the type of restaurant you're running. I tell my crew that we just want to be the best example of *X*. We want to be the best BYOB in the city. We want to be the best fine dining. We want to be the best date night. We want to be the best of everything. And if we feel like we're slacking in any category, we push.

HOW TO USE THIS BOOK

Recipes from four tasting menus, one from each season, fill the following pages. Each features eight savory courses, a dessert, and a complementary cocktail from our bar next door, In the Valley. Together they form blueprints for re-creating a Laurel tasting menu at home. They're designed to give you the flow and balance in flavors, temperatures, and textures we engineer at the restaurant, so if you've got the time and ambition, I would highly encourage you to prepare a whole menu and throw a kickass dinner party (and please invite me). Obviously that won't work for everyone, so while these recipes are designed to complement one another, each can also stand on its own. Page through the book and see what jumps out at you. Want to learn how to process a whole lobe of foie gras (page 21), or bond black-trumpet stuffing to a butterflied Dover sole (page 72)? We've got you. Or maybe the gnocchi that are my daughter Grace's favorite (page 70) are more your speed. Different recipes—and the recipes *within* the recipes—throughout this book cover skill levels that range from beginner to very proficient, and it's perfectly okay to cherry-pick. As a professional chef and habitual cookbook buyer, I have always thought that a cookbook was worth buying if I get one idea or one recipe out of it. I think of it as improving my repertoire, $30 to $50 at a time.

MEASUREMENTS AND TIMING

The recipes included in this book are real dishes that we cook at Laurel, and they are authentic with regard to how they're made at the restaurant, which usually means according to metric measurements. We weigh almost everything in grams, but in transcribing our recipes from dozens of black Moleskines for this project, we've also included their American conversions.

Every dish we serve at Laurel has multiple and sometimes time-consuming components, and since our kitchen is about the size of a walk-in closet, we have to be strategic about how we utilize time and space. So apples roast for thirty-six hours in a barely warm oven; onion tops can spend half a day in the dehydrator; lamb saddles take twenty-two days of hanging to cure; proteins circulate sous vide overnight. Hang around our kitchen in the afternoon and there's a high probability you'll hear, "Siri, set timer for seventy-two hours." Please read a recipe in its entirety before starting to cook it in order to determine the schedule best suited to your kitchen (and your life). Except where it makes sense to do otherwise, we've written these recipes starting with the component that takes the most time, progressing to the component that takes the least. The

upside to this method is that almost everything can be made in advance and then finished to order in less than ten minutes (as described in the "To Plate" portion of each recipe), which is exactly how we do it at the restaurant.

Our master recipes are batched out in portions of ten, fifteen, and twenty, because that's how they're best suited to our space and our reservation book. Because that's not the case for the home cook, we've scaled the majority of the recipes down to the number that suits each best. With some exceptions, smaller courses like the Wellfleet Oyster Cream (page 102) are typically scaled for four or six, while the heartier, protein-driven courses like Braised Lamb Neck (page 114) are portioned for two or four. Some dishes require components that can't be scaled down in a meaningful way—try making just a tablespoon of black raspberry preserves, duck jus, or chive oil—and in those cases you'll have some leftovers. Fortunately, black raspberry preserves, duck jus, and chive oil are delicious on lots of other things not in this book. This also goes for pickles and ferments, which we usually prepare in one-pound batches. Store leftovers in the fridge for future snacking.

INGREDIENTS

Although we focus on seasonal ingredients, our menus don't so much represent moments in the Mid-Atlantic as they are mosaics of what our farmers are growing in a given week, what our foragers are harvesting from seashores and woods, and what we've preserved through canning, pickling, fermentation, and dehydration throughout the growing season. Each recipe is presented the way we make it, right down to the apple blossoms, bachelor's buttons, and Olio Verde, the Sicilian extra-virgin I keep in a squeeze bottle at my station to finish certain dishes. Appropriate substitutions are noted throughout the book. As for pantry ingredients, a new generation of accomplished home cooks has forced food stores to up their game. Things like agar-agar, xanthan gum, canned Burgundy snails, and bottled yuzu juice are easier than ever to source. If all else fails, order online.

SHOPPING LIST:

Activa: An enzyme that binds amino acids in proteins. Its generic name is active transglutanimase, but it often goes by the nickname "meat glue."

Agar-agar: A seaweed-based hydrocolloid used for gelling.

Black garlic: Garlic that has been cooked very slowly so that the sugars have caramelized. We buy this ingredient, but we also make our own versions with other alliums like shallots (page 161) and garlic scapes (page 144).

Burgundy snails: Snails from Burgundy, France, sold cooked and canned. These are the most consistently beautiful and tender escargots I've ever had.

Citric acid: A powder derived from isolating the acidic compounds of citrus fruit.

Cremodan 30: An ice cream and sorbet stabilizer containing locust bean gum, monoglycerides, guar gum, and carrageenan.

Feuille de brik: A sturdy, crepe-like dough that crisps up very well. It is sold in large sheets.

Gelatin: An animal-based thickener in powdered or sheet form. It comes in bronze, silver, gold, and platinum grades, each creating a stiffer gel than the last. We use silver sheets for all of our recipes.

Glucose syrup: Glucose is a simple sugar that is less sweet than white sugar (which is a mixture of the two sugars glucose and fructose). In America, glucose syrup is predominantly made with corn.

Isomalt: A sugar substitute that's a sugar alcohol. It typically comes in powdered or pebbled form.

Kasu: The residual yeast, or lees, left over from making sake. It has a strong fermented-rice flavor.

Koji: Inoculated fermented rice used to make everything from sake to miso. We use it in extract and vinegar forms.

Malic acid: An isolated acid derived from apples.

Seaweeds: We use dried kombu for enhancing many of our stocks, though the Bourbon-Glazed Grilled Lobster (page 66) calls for bladderwrack, a fresh seaweed harvested along the Atlantic. We also use liquid kelp extract.

Tapioca maltodextrin: We use this starchy thickener to stabilize and disperse fats when making powders or crisps.

Tartaric acid: Cream of tartar, a versatile ingredient derived predominantly from grapes that can be used in leavening, souring, and as an antioxidant.

Trimoline: An inverted sugar derived predominantly from beets.

Truffle jus: Liquid derived from fermented truffles. We buy it from D'Artagnan.

Ultra-Tex 8: A hydrocolloid derived from tapioca root.

Versawhip: A modified soy protein used as a substitute for eggs in whipping.

Vin jaune: French wine made from late-harvest Sauvignon Blanc grapes.

White soy sauce: A lighter, more delicately flavored soy sauce, made with a greater ratio of wheat to soy.

Yuzu: A distinctive Japanese citrus fruit that's not typically eaten; the juice and the rind have many applications. We use bottled juice most often.

Xanthan gum: A vegetable-based thickening agent. We often thicken sauces with xanthan to reduce the amount of butter used and for the better flavor release it facilitates.

A short glossary of plants and produce also appears in the back of the book.

- - - - - - - - -

Here are some ingredient standards that apply to the recipes unless otherwise specified:

- Butter is unsalted.

- Milk is whole.

- Eggs are large.

- Olive oil is extra-virgin, your preferred brand. Olio Verde, my favorite, is called for specifically throughout the book to finish certain dishes.

- Salt is Diamond Crystal kosher salt. Do not use Morton's; the food will turn out twice as salty. Other salts that appear in this book include Maldon sea salt for finishing, and curing salt for charcuterie.

- Sugar is white granulated. Light and dark brown sugars, caster sugar, and sanding sugar also appear in this book and are indicated by name.

- Citrus juices are freshly squeezed. The only exception is yuzu juice, which we buy bottled. All zest is freshly grated.

- Flowers, herbs, and garnishes are fresh.

- Fruits and vegetables are medium in size, washed, and peeled. For items that run extra dirty, like mushrooms, daylilies, celery root, and some other foraged plants, additional cleaning may be noted in the process.

- Except for boiling, all water we use is filtered, since Philly tap water runs high in calcium.

EQUIPMENT

You might see an unfamiliar piece of equipment listed here or there throughout the book, but don't worry—I don't expect you to run out and buy a Pacojet. With very few exceptions, all of these recipes can be made with everyday kitchen gear. Here are some general notes to consider.

Vacuum Bags and Sealers

You'll often see a recipe call for vacuum bags. These are the plastic bags that go with our sealer, which combines ingredients in an oxygen-free environment. We use the sealer for four techniques: (1) compressing the flavor of one ingredient into another, as in the Marigold-Compressed Kohlrabi (page 132), (2) fermenting, (3) pickling, and (4) prepping ingredients to cook sous vide in a water bath. There are two types of sealers on the market. A chamber sealer is what we use at the restaurant (and also what you'll find in most professional kitchens), and it works for all these techniques. The FoodSaver and similar versions are smaller, less expensive, and widely available, but they only work for two of the four techniques: fermenting and sous vide. Since compressing and pickling involve wet ingredients, you need a chamber sealer, which is compatible with liquids. The FoodSaver will suck some or all of the liquid out of the bag, even on the wet/moist setting, but it works fine for fermentation and for sealing ingredients for water-bath cooking. For compressing without a chamber sealer, the closest approximation is macerating the ingredients together for thirty-six hours. You won't change the texture of the fruit or vegetable, but you will get some flavor in there. To pickle without a chamber sealer, just use the traditional crock or glass jar method people have been using for centuries. We use bags at the restaurant to save space. And if you don't have a sealer, here's a cool hack: Grab a sturdy zip-top plastic bag, the kind with the little plastic zipper at the top, fill it with the ingredients, and slowly lower it into a pot of water while it is still open. As you lower it, the surrounding water pressure will naturally compress the ingredients in the bag and expel the air. Lower the bag until the zipper is just above the surface of the water, then seal.

	CHAMBER	FOODSAVER	NO SEALER
Compressing	✓	Macerate	Macerate
Pickling	✓	Traditional pickle	Traditional pickle
Fermenting	✓	✓	Water-pressure hack
Sous Vide Cooking	✓	✓	Water-pressure hack

Each recipe that involves vacuum sealing will specify a bag size of small, medium, or large, and whether to seal on low or high. Each sealer model is different, so consult your manual. Ours counts down from sixty seconds. For low seal we stop the process at forty-five seconds. For high seal we let it count all the way down. I'm pretty sure we have the ability to preprogram these settings, but we've never gotten around to doing so (or have never been able to figure it out), so my chef de cuisine, Eddie Konrad, and I usually just stare at it and count.

Sous Vide Cooking and Immersion Circulators

While you can often get around the need for a vacuum sealer, there's no easy way to substitute for the control and precision you can achieve with an immersion circulator. We cook most of our proteins at Laurel sous vide at least partway, so many of the recipes in this book reflect that. If you don't have one already, there are several easy-to-use immersion circulators on the market designed for home cooks. Anova's model attaches to any deep pot and costs less than $100, a worthwhile investment you'll wind up using even when you're not cooking from this book.

Dehydrator

We dehydrate a lot—and I'm not talking about getting thirsty during service. Onion tops, strawberries, mushrooms, and garlic scapes are just few of the things that get dried in our Excalibur dehydrator. This lets us preserve foods from other seasons, create new textures, and turn waste into something usable and delicious. If you have a dehydrator, great. If not, your oven set to its lowest temperature can perform the same function. Arrange whatever you want to dehydrate on a wire rack set into a sheet pan, and leave it in the oven anywhere from twelve to twenty-four hours, but consult independent recipes before getting started. Note that the recipes for Black Garlic Scapes (page 144) and Black Shallots (page 161) would tie up your oven for three weeks, which is obviously not feasible unless you happen to be on a raw diet. An electric dehydrator will be significantly less obtrusive. "Black" alliums can also be made in a rice cooker.

Smoker

Occasionally you'll see recipes that call for smoking ingredients, like the fish bones in our Smoked-Mackerel Dashi (page 128). At the restaurant we do all our smoking in the backyard in a contraption Eddie hooked up using a stockpot, a small Weber grill, and a dryer vent. If you have a charcoal grill at home, you can convert it into a smoker with soaked woodchips—we typically use apple and cherry—or you can pick up a Breville/PolyScience Smoking Gun, a handheld device that lets you easily smoke foods through a rubber hose.

Pacojet

A Pacojet is like a giant drill with a sharp blade that creates super-tight purées and beautiful ice creams and custards with microscopic ice crystals. Every other restaurant I worked at wouldn't let me get one, so when I opened Laurel it was the first thing I bought with my own money. Only three recipes in this book use a Pacojet, so I don't recommend running out to buy one unless you have a lot of cash and a serious homemade ice cream habit. A pretty convincing version of horseradish snow in the Albacore Crudo (page 116) can be made like a granite (see Lovage Granite, page 116), and the raw-milk ice cream in the Honeysuckle-Poached Rhubarb dessert (page 116) and the Salsify Ice Cream in the Paddlefish Caviar with Vodka Cream (page 136) can be made in a standard electric ice cream maker.

iSi Gun

The iSi gun is great for making seltzer and whipped cream, but we use it at Laurel mostly for mousses (we try not to say *foams*, a term that is often held up, unfairly, as the cliché of the molecular gastronomy movement) that are very intense in flavor but super light and airy in texture. Charged with nitrous oxide, the iSi keeps mousses stable throughout service, allowing us to dispense them to order as we plate, instead of having to whip them à la minute. The iSi runs about $90, but there are other brands for less than $50 (search for whipped cream dispensers).

Liquid Nitrogen

We use liquid nitrogen to flash-freeze things we want to powder, especially oily items like nuts, which normally turn into paste when you purée them. Hit them with nitro, and they flash freeze and can be buzzed into dry particles. We also use liquid nitrogen for our bread and butter service. We make our own butter and drop little pieces of it into nitro, so they come out like butter Dippin' Dots. If you want to work with nitro at home, you need to purchase it from a certified distributor in your area (usually a welding supply company), have a special storage container called a dewar, and take extreme caution (gloves, goggles) when using it.

Sieve v. Chinois

Throughout the book we call for passing purées, stocks, and other ingredients through a sieve or chinois, both of which are types of strainers. A sieve or china cap has medium holes through which liquids will easily strain, while the chinois is lined in a fine mesh that's better for achieving a perfectly smooth texture, like you want with the caramelized sunchoke purée in the Duck Breast with Blackberry and Chicory Crumble (page 134).

Here's a list of other gear you might consider picking up:

- Stainless-steel mesh-lid shakers, for dusting powders

- Plastic squeeze bottles, for holding and applying purées and sauces

- Tweezers, for delicate garnishes

- Silicone spherical ice molds, for making ice for cocktails.

STAFF

Tonight We Are Serving

I.
Apple-Yuzu Consommé,
Marinated Trout Roe, Bitter Greens

II.
Albacore Crudo, Horseradish Snow, Pears

III.
Sea Urchin, Creamed Corn,
Sunflower-Truffle Vinaigrette

IV.
Frozen Foie Gras Tarte, Elderberry Vinegar,
Black Raspberry, Hibiscus

V.
Burgundy Snails, Onion,
Mushrooms, Potato Chips

VI.
Grilled Mackerel, Black Garlic Tuile,
Smoked-Mackerel Dashi

VII.
Burnt-Sugar Salsify, Cured Lamb,
Black Trumpets, Watercress

VIII.
Duck Breast, Caramelized Sunchoke,
Blackberry, Chicory Crumble

IX.
Roasted Apple, Caramel-Coffee Cream,
Black Walnut, Apple Wine

X.
Cocktail: Drunken Farmer

III.

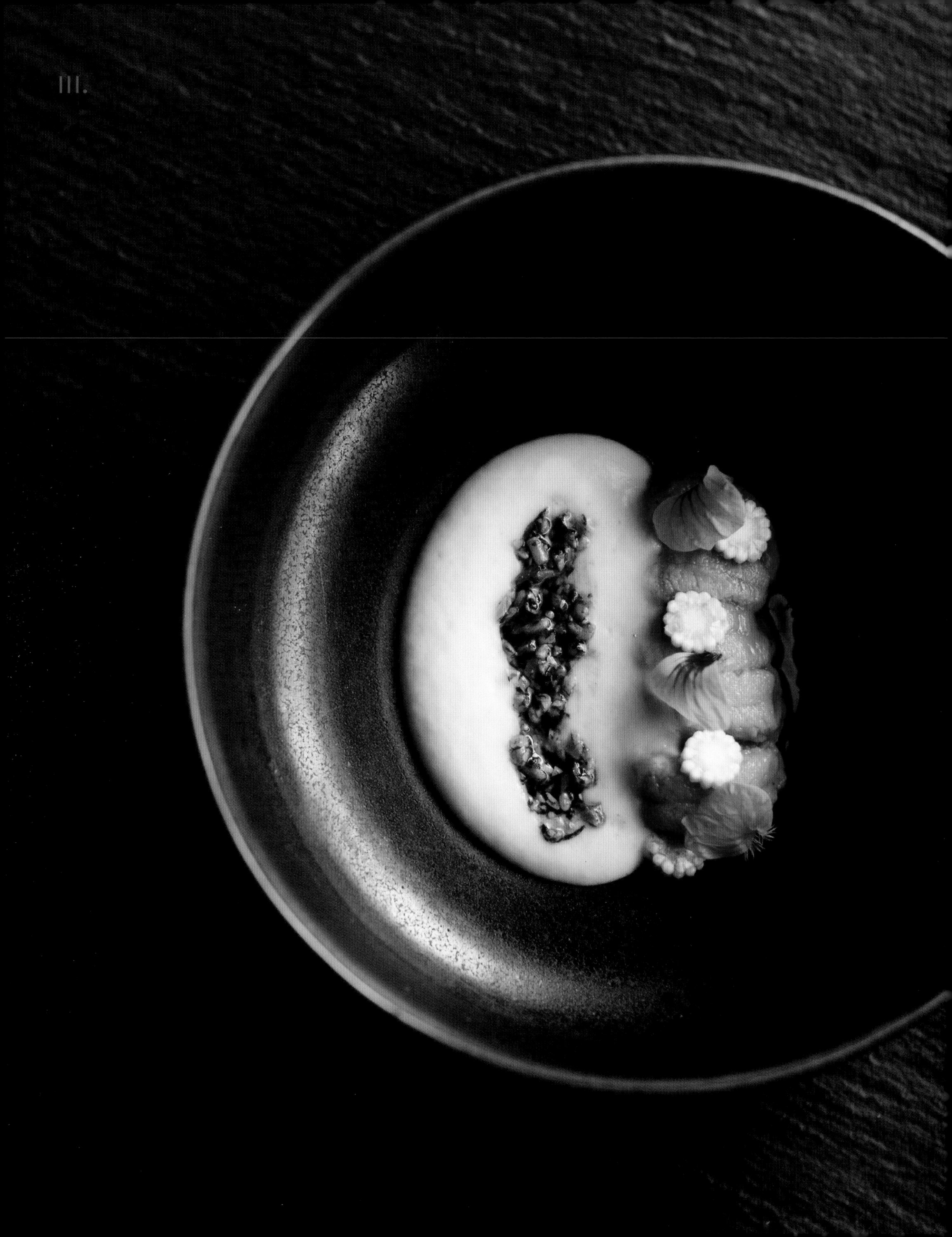

V.

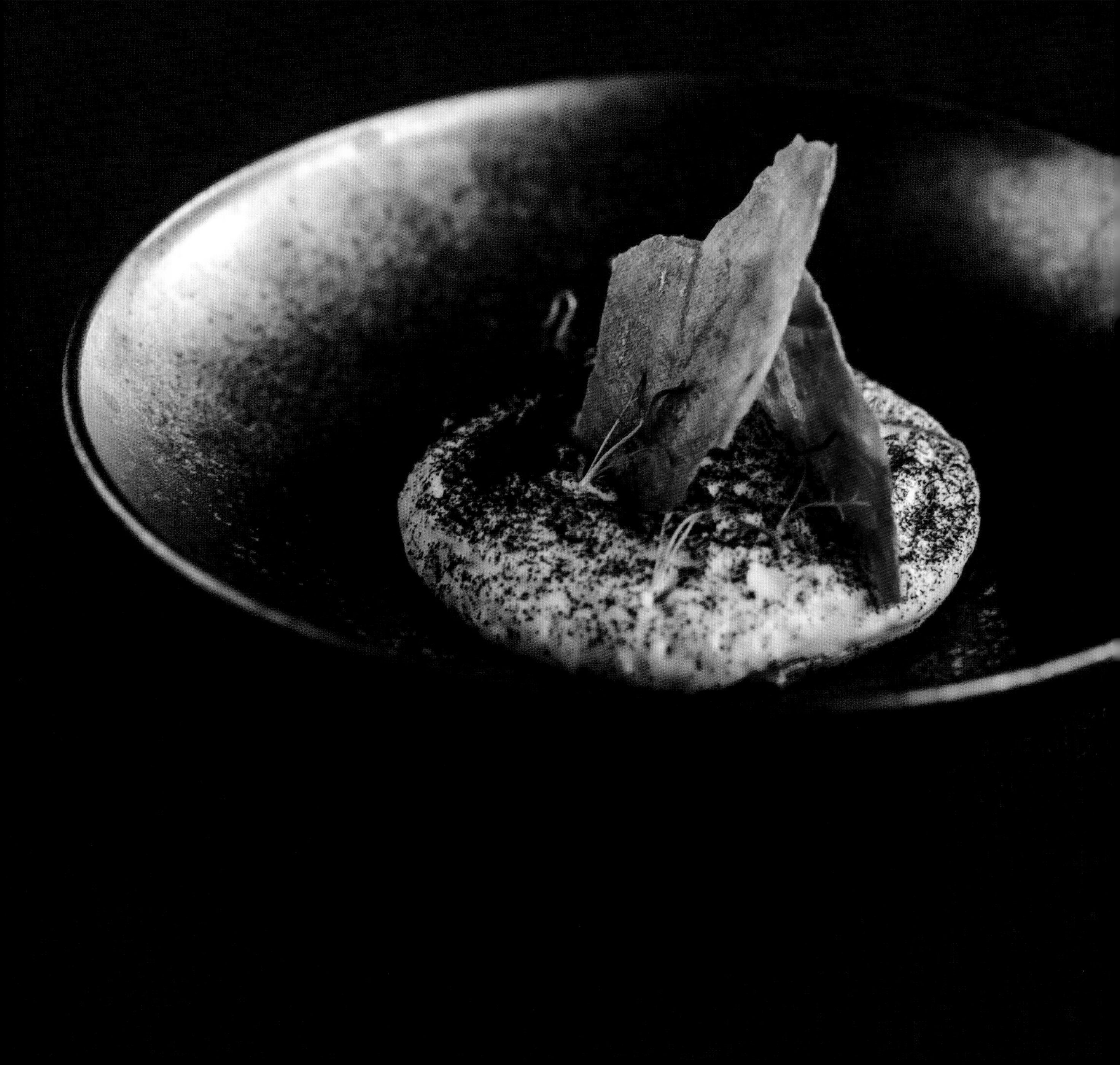

APPLE-YUZU CONSOMMÉ, MARINATED TROUT ROE, BITTER GREENS

Green apples are a very Mid-Atlantic, this-is-who-we-are ingredient. Each season here you get one great fruit or vegetable that's full of acid, and in the fall it's the green apple. I've loved sour stuff since I was a kid, and this dish has an unbelievable brightness that activates your entire tongue. I've been doing a version of it since our first year at Laurel, but the essence of this variation, the consommé, comes from when I was working at Oceana in New York in 2003. Back then, it was all about clarifying liquids with gelatin through a freeze-thaw process, which takes forever. Now we use agar-agar, which has the same clarifying properties but works in a fraction of the time. Green apples are great, green apple juice is better, and clarified green apple juice seasoned with a little bit of yuzu is absolutely spectacular. The trick here is capturing that flavor in the consommé, then delivering it in two different textures in the same dish. So you have it as a gelée (with salty trout roe, fresh diced green apple, and chives) on the bottom and as an airy emulsion (dusted with fermented scallion powder) over top. Anytime we can take a familiar ingredient and introduce it in a different texture, that's worth exploring.

MAKES 4 PORTIONS

APPLE-YUZU CONSOMMÉ

32.5 ounces/1,000 g fresh Granny Smith apple juice
1.4 ounces/40 g yuzu juice
.6 ounce/10 g lime juice
Pinch of Kosher salt
.5 ounce/15 g granulated sugar
⅓ teaspoon/1 g agar-agar

Combine the juices, salt, and sugar in a mixing bowl. Whisk until the salt and sugar are dissolved. Pour 7 ounces/200 g of the seasoned juice into a small pot with the agar, and emulsify, using an immersion blender. Bring the mix to a simmer over medium heat and simmer for 2 minutes, continually whisking. Combine with the remaining juice by whisking the warm mixture slowly into the cool mixture. Allow it to cool over ice for an hour to set; it will look like a slushy. Gently break up the mixture with a whisk, and slowly pour it through 5 layers of cheesecloth. Reserve the consommé cold.

APPLE-YUZU GELÉE

7 ounces/200 g Apple-Yuzu Consommé
1.5 sheets silver gelatin

Gently warm the consommé to 90°F in a small pot. Soak the gelatin in ice water for 10 minutes. Strain the gelatin, and squeeze out any excess water. Melt the gelatin into the warm consommé. Strain through a chinois into a small container. Let the gelatin set for at least 6 hours. Break up the consommé with a whisk and reserve cold.

WHIPPED APPLE

4 sheets silver gelatin
12.7 ounces/360 g Apple-Yuzu Consommé
3.5 ounces/100 g granulated sugar
4 egg whites

Soak the gelatin in ice water for 10 minutes.

Use an immersion blender to combine the consommé and the sugar. Warm the mixture to 170°F or until the sugar has dissolved.

Remove the gelatin from the ice water and squeeze out any excess water. Add the egg whites and soaked gelatin to the consommé, and emulsify quickly with an immersion blender. Pass through a chinois, and pour into an iSi container. Charge three times with CO_2, shaking each time in between. Let the container sit for at least 2 hours in the refrigerator.

TO PLATE

2 tablespoons/32 g trout roe
½ Granny Smith apple, brunoised
1 tablespoon/2 g minced chive
Chive Oil (see page 163)
Bitter Greens Purée (see page 163)
Fermented Scallion Powder (see page 161)

Place the trout roe, apple, chives, and 1 tablespoon/8 g chive oil in a small bowl. Mix gently to avoid breaking the roe. Spoon 1 teaspoon/5 g of the bitter greens purée into the center of a serving bowl. Cover the purée with 1 tablespoon/5 g of the apple-yuzu gelée. Cover half the gelée with a quarter of the roe-apple mix. Foam a quarter of the whipped apple over the other half of the gelée, leveling gently with an offset spatula to make a clean dividing line. Dust a quarter of the scallion powder over the whipped apple. Repeat for the remaining three portions.

ALBACORE CRUDO, HORSERADISH SNOW, PEARS

When we were developing Laurel, my business partner, Jonathan Cohen, and I would meet for lunch at Famous Fourth Street, an iconic deli in Queen Village. The fish in horseradish cream they do there wasn't something I thought I would be into, but as soon as I tasted it I knew I had to try replicate those flavors in a dish of my own. Here, we replace less flavorful whiting with albacore tuna, which has the fattiness to stand up to powerful horseradish. Albacore is an underutilized fish that has a bright acidity I like a lot. We perform this great trick: poaching it at one hundred degrees to firm up the flesh a little bit while the fish still looks dead raw. If you can't find high-quality albacore, this recipe works well with other varieties of tuna.

MAKES 4 PORTIONS

HORSERADISH SNOW

14 ounces/400 g sour cream
1 ounce/30 g granulated sugar
1.5 ounces/40 g yuzu juice
4.5 ounces/130 g freshly grated horseradish
1 teaspoon/5 g Kosher salt
1 teaspoon/3 g agar-agar
12.3 ounces/350 g water

Combine the sour cream, sugar, yuzu juice, horserad-ish, and salt in a large bowl.

Combine the agar and the water in a small pot, and bring to a simmer, stirring to dissolve the agar, about 2 minutes. Add the dissolved agar to the bowl with the sour cream mixture and stir gently. Load the blend into a Pacojet container. Freeze overnight, and process in the Pacojet the following day. Alternately, you can make a close approximation of the snow using the same method as you would for a traditional granite: Transfer the mix to a shallow pan, and place in the freezer. Every half hour, scrape the surface with a fork to create ice crystals. Repeat until the entire mixture is frozen and fluffy.

ALBACORE CRUDO

1 pound/454 g trimmed sushi-grade albacore
    tuna loin
Kosher salt
Grated zest of 1 yuzu
2 ounces/56 g extra-virgin olive oil

Cut the tuna into two bars measuring 3 inches long, 1 inch wide, and 1 inch tall. Season the fish liberally with salt and yuzu zest. Transfer to a medium vacuum bag with the olive oil, seal on high, and let the fish "cure" in the fridge for 2 hours. Meanwhile, set a circulator to 100°F. Poach the fish in the bag for 25 minutes to set the texture. Cool the bagged fish in a bowl of ice water. Once cooled, remove from the bag and reserve cold.

PEAR PURÉE

2 Asian pears, cored and halved
1 tablespoon/15 g extra-virgin olive oil
1 teaspoon/2 g citric acid
1½ teaspoons/4 g xanthan gum

Set a circulator to 185°F. Combine the pears, olive oil, and citric acid in a small vacuum bag, and seal on low. Cook sous vide for 45 minutes. Strain the pears and discard the liquid. Purée the cooked pears with the xanthan, and strain through a chinois into a plastic squeeze bottle for serving.

TO PLATE

½ cored Asian pear, shaved into thin slices and cut into triangles
24 mustard flowers

Set 4 pieces of tuna in the center of a shallow bowl. Top with 2 dots of pear purée and 6 slices of Asian pear. Cover the tuna completely with horseradish snow. Garnish with 6 mustard flowers. Repeat for the remaining portions. Cut each bar of tuna into 4 equal cubes, then slice each cube on a bias into triangles, for a total of 16 pieces.

SEA URCHIN, CREAMED CORN, SUNFLOWER-TRUFFLE VINAIGRETTE

Uni is the attention-grabber in this course, but the genesis of the dish actually lies in a bottle of Togo-Su kurozu, a brown-rice koji vinegar that's been made in Japan for two hundred years. It has this wild flavor that reminds me of Dr. Pepper with a shiitake finish, which we amplify with truffles, adding texture with sunflower seeds. We loved this vinaigrette and were thinking about what it would complement. A lot of our food at Laurel comes together this way, starting with one ingredient or component then building a focused plate around it; a dish rarely comes to life in its first iteration. So we began with shellfish, then went to sea urchin, then thought, What goes well with sea urchin? Corn.

My in-laws are huge history buffs—stay with me—and they visit Williamsburg, Virginia, probably three or four times a year. I was looking through my father-in-law's Williamsburg cookbook while we were working on this dish at the restaurant. He makes a delicious corn pudding from a recipe in that book. Inspired by that dish, we tried individual corn puddings topped with uni and the vinaigrette, but the texture was too creamy-on-creamy. By using an iSi gun we were able to change the corn element from a pudding to a light mousse, which successfully altered the texture while still preserving the rich corn flavor that pairs so well with the urchin, truffles, koji, and sunflower seeds.

When sourcing sea urchin, keep in mind that they vary in size and flavor across the species. Maine uni is different from Santa Barbara uni is different from Hokkaido uni—so on and so forth. What we use depends on what's coming in fresh from our fish purveyors. This recipe was tested with Maine urchin, which tend to be smaller and have more of an iron flavor than what you find on the West Coast. You can use whichever urchin you prefer, but for larger specimens you should reduce the portion from five pieces per person to three.

CREAMED-CORN MOUSSE

36 ounces/1 kg corn kernels
27 ounces/750 g heavy whipping cream
14 ounces/400 g whole milk
.5 ounce/14 g agar-agar
.75 ounce/21 g Kosher salt

Combine the corn, cream, and milk in a large pot. Simmer very gently for 30 minutes over low heat—you want to avoid reducing the liquid. Whisk in the agar, and remove the pot from the heat. Transfer the mixture to a shallow pan, and place over a bowl of ice to cool and set, about 30 minutes. Once the liquid sets, purée the mixture, and add the salt. Warm 1 quart of the puréed corn in a saucepan over medium heat, and transfer to an iSi gun. Charge with two N_2O canisters; reserve, submerged halfway in a 165°F circulator bath, until plating.

SUNFLOWER-TRUFFLE VINAIGRETTE

2.25 ounces/64 g chopped sunflower seeds, toasted
1 ounce/30 g preserved truffle paste
1.2 ounces/38 g koji vinegar
2.5 ounces/70 g extra-virgin olive oil
Kosher salt

Combine the sunflower seeds, truffle paste, vinegar, and olive oil in a bowl. Stir together with a spoon, and add salt to taste. Reserve at room temperature.

TO PLATE

Uni from 2 to 3 fresh large sea urchins (about 3.5 ounces/99 grams)
Pickled Baby Corn (see page 159)
Nasturtium flowers

Spoon 1 teaspoon of sunflower vinaigrette into the bottom of a small bowl. Arrange five pieces of urchin in a row on top of the vinaigrette. Shake the iSi gun, and dispense about ½ cup/125 g of the creamed-corn mousse on top of the vinaigrette; don't cover the urchin. Garnish with 4 slices of pickled baby corn and 3 nasturtium petals. Top the mousse with a few drops of additional vinaigrette. Repeat for remaining portions.

FROZEN FOIE GRAS TARTE, ELDERBERRY VINEGAR, BLACK RASPBERRY, HIBISCUS

When we go out to eat, my wife mentions one thing when the server asks if there are any allergies or aversions: foie gras. The richness and creaminess of foie, the way it takes over your palate, just isn't her thing. And I hear that. At Le Bec-Fin, we used to do a whole roasted lobe of foie or a giant torchon as its own course, which was luxury overkill. I think less is more with foie; its flavor is more powerful in a one-bite dish, which is what we do in this snack. The taste goal was to deliver foie flavor that was focused but not domineering. The texture goal was to do it in a way that my wife would enjoy.

To accomplish these tasks, we looked to the freezer. One thing I love about foie is its temperature versatility. You can serve it as a hot liquid at 110°F, a mousse at 50°F to 70°F, a torchon at 35°F to 50°F, or frozen below 30°F. Each application has a different texture and flavor release, and frozen is the most ephemeral. Shaved into fine curls with a bench scraper, frozen foie gras melts in your mouth and disappears. We pile the shavings into brittle tart shells and add elements of preserved berries and hibiscus, so in a single bite you get crunch, acid, sweetness, and that final note of foie. And then it's gone. My wife approves.

Foie gras can be challenging to work with, but we've found a way to cut 24 hours out of the process. Instead of following the standard method (soaking foie in milk, then ice water, then curing it for a couple of days), we brine it for a day, which takes care of the soaking and curing steps in one shot. Then all you need to do is pass it through a chinois, freeze it, and make the curls with a bench scraper. This recipe will leave you with extra foie shavings; store them in the freezer in a nonreactive, airtight container between layers of parchment. Stir them into bowls of warm grain, melt them into pan sauces, sprinkle them over vanilla ice cream, or just snack on them right from the container.

BLACK RASPBERRY PURÉE

2 pounds/900 g black raspberries
1 pint/450 ml rosé wine vinegar
1 cup/220 g granulated sugar
1 pint/450 ml water
1 teaspoon/2 g citric acid
Agar-agar, as needed

Combiner the berries, vinegar, sugar, water, and citric acid in a medium pot. Bring to a simmer, remove from the heat, and cover. Let the mixture stand for 20 minutes. Strain it through a fine sieve, and discard the seeds. Weigh the remaining liquid. It should be between 1,500 and 1,700 grams. Multiply this number by .01. The result should be between 15 and 17. Weigh out agar in that number of grams. For example, if the raspberry liquid weighs 1,587 grams, you'll use 15.87 grams of agar. Use an immersion blender to emulsify the agar into the raspberry liquid. Pour the liquid into a clean pot and bring to a simmer, constantly whisking. Continue to whisk and simmer for 2 minutes, until thickened. Remove from heat, transfer the emulsion to a clean container, and refrigerate until cold and set firm, about 1 hour. Purée in a blender until smooth, pass through a sieve, and reserve in a plastic squeeze bottle for serving.

TARTE SHELLS

2 sheets feuille de brik, 8 inches/20 cm each
3 tablespoons/45 g unsalted butter, melted

Preheat the oven to 325°F. Using a 2.5-inch/6.4-cm round pastry cutter, punch out 8 rounds of feuille de brik per sheet (16 rounds total). Discard the trim. As you work, keep the rounds covered with a damp napkin so they don't dry out. Have two mini muffin tins ready. Working quickly, brush the rounds of dough on both sides with melted butter, and stack them in twos, for a total of 8 stacked rounds. Flip one of the muffin tins upside down. Brush the bottom of the muffin tin with melted butter, and place each stacked round of dough on top of an inverted muffin cup. Brush the inside of the second mini muffin tin with melted butter, and gently but quickly place it over the stacks of dough so that the feuille is compressed between the two muffin tins. Keeping the muffin tins inverted, bake for 15 minutes. Remove from the oven, and immediately remove the top tin. Use an offset spatula to gently pry the tarte shells from the bottom tin. Let them cool to room temperature. Store the shells, covered, in a nonreactive airtight container in a dry and cool place.

FROZEN FOIE GRAS

2 pounds/900 g fresh A- or B-grade foie gras
1 quart/1 L Meat Brine (see page 158)
Kosher salt

Rinse the foie gras well, and cut it into large cubes. Divide the cubes between 2 large vacuum bags, and cover the foie gras with the brine. Seal the bags on high, and reserve cold for 24 hours. The following day, strain off the brine and rinse the foie gras. Leave the foie out at room temperature, covered, until it is soft like putty. Pass it through a fine chinois with a plastic bench scraper. Taste the foie for seasoning, and add salt if needed. Place the foie gras in a 14 x 12-inch/36 x 30-cm pan. Tap the pan a few times on the counter to remove any air pockets. Cover the foie with plastic wrap, and freeze it for 24 hours. Remove it from the freezer. Position the pan against a wall so it doesn't slide away from you. Holding a metal bench scraper with two hands, scrape off the top layer of foie. Place the frozen foie curls in a clean container, and cover them with a layer of parchment. Continue the scraping and layering process until you have enough curls to fill your tarte molds, about 2 ounces/57 g total. Reserve in the freezer, covered, until serving.

ELDERBERRY VINEGAR GEL

2.5 sheets silver gelatin
8 ounces/250 g Elderberry Vinegar (see page 159)
4 teaspoons/18 g granulated sugar
Pinch of Kosher salt

Place the gelatin in ice-cold water to hydrate. Meanwhile, warm the vinegar in a medium saucepan to 145°F. Add the sugar and salt, and stir to dissolve. Remove the gelatin from the water, and squeeze out any excess water. Add the gelatin to the vinegar, and stir to melt completely. Transfer to a nonreactive airtight container, and place in the refrigerator to set for about 2 hours.

TO PLATE

Powdered hibiscus in a shaker
Freeze-dried elderberries

Working quickly, squeeze a small dot of the preserved black raspberry into the bottom of each tarte shell. Cover with a teaspoon of the elderberry vinegar gel. Remove the foie from the freezer, and break up the pieces if necessary with a spoon. Overfill each tarte shell with the frozen foie curls. Dust each tarte lightly with the powdered hibiscus, and garnish with a freeze-dried elderberry. Serve immediately.

BURGUNDY SNAILS, ONION, MUSHROOMS, POTATO CHIPS

I never liked snails until I started working at Le Bec-Fin. There, we poached them for six hours in a court bouillon with Chartreuse, a liqueur that picks up on the snails' subtle anise undertone, and served them with a very, very strong garlic-shallot-parsley butter. At Laurel, we don't cook ours for six hours—the beautiful Burgundy specimens we get from Doug "The Snail Man" Dussault come cooked and canned, great for restaurant kitchens and home cooks—but we do throw back to that old-school French flavor profile I first loved at Le Bec, with spring onion tops, garlic, butter, and, of course, a swig of Chartreuse. We also introduce shiitake mushrooms; not only does the flavor work well with the snails, but the texture is similar, so as you get into the dish you almost don't know which you're eating. This is how we convert a lot of snail doubters. We haven't been able to take it off the menu.

ONION PURÉE, PICKLES, AND DUST

10 spring onions, tops and bulbs separated, scraps from trimming reserved
1 teaspoon/4.5g kosher salt
1 quart/1 L Sweet Pickle Brine (see page 158)

To make the purée, blanch the tops in boiling, well-salted water for 4 minutes. Transfer the tops to ice water to stop the cooking and set the color. When fully cooled, strain, squeezing out the excess water. Purée in a blender with the salt to form a very smooth paste. Transfer to a plastic squeeze bottle and reserve cold.

For the pickled onions, bring the brine to a boil, remove from heat, and allow to cool. Use a mandoline to slice the onion bulbs very thin. Place the onions in a large vacuum bag, and add enough cooled brine to cover. Seal on high, and refrigerate for 2 days.

Place whatever scraps you have from trimming the onions in a deep pan, and cover with aluminum foil. Bake at 375°F for 12 to 18 hours or until completely black and charred. Use a spice grinder to turn the charred onions into a fine powder. Reserve in a mesh-top shaker at room temperature.

POTATO EMULSION

17.6 ounces/500 g Yukon Gold potatoes, peeled and diced large
17.6 ounces/500 g whole milk
17.6 ounces/500 g heavy whipping cream
3.5 ounces/100 g unsalted butter

Place the potatoes, milk, cream, and butter in a large pot. Cover with a cartouche. Bring to a very low simmer, and cook for about an hour or until the potatoes are very tender. Use a thermometer to monitor the temperature; it should never exceed 195°F. Strain the potatoes, reserving the liquid. Pass the potatoes through a ricer. Using an immersion blender, purée the liquid back into the potatoes. Place the warm liquid in a large iSi container, and charge twice with NO_2. Reserve warm by submerging the container halfway in 165°F water.

POTATO SHEETS

5 large Yukon Gold potatoes
1 pound/453 g clarified butter, melted
Kosher salt
4 ounces/125 g potato starch, in a shaker

Preheat the oven to 300°F. Line a full sheet tray with a silicone baking mat. Peel the potatoes and submerge them in ice water to prevent oxidation. Cut ½ inch/1.3 cm from both sides of the long ends of the potato. Using a vegetable sheeter, cut thin, long sheets of potato, and place them back in the ice water.

Brush the baking mat with clarified butter. Strain the potato sheets and pat them dry. Arrange a single layer of potato on the baking sheet, making sure to overlap the pieces. If necessary, trim them so that they fill the entire tray. Brush the potato strips with butter, season with salt, and shake an even layer of potato starch on top. Quickly cut and arrange another layer of potato on top, overlapping to make small seams and pressing down to remove air bubbles. Brush with butter, season with salt, and dust with starch. Repeat a third time. Lay another silicone baking mat on top of the giant "potato chip." Weigh it down with a second full sheet tray. Bake for 10 minutes. Remove the top sheet tray and the top silicone mat. Bake for an additional 20 minutes or until deep golden and very crisp. Remove the potato chip from the sheet tray, and set aside in a cool place.

SNAIL RAGOUT

24 large wild Burgundy snails
1 pound/453 g shiitake mushrooms, cleaned, caps
      and stems separated
1 quart/1 L water
3 tablespoons/45 g extra-virgin olive oil
1 white onion, finely diced
6 garlic cloves, minced
1 cup/250 ml pinot grigio
4 ounces/125 g green Chartreuse
Kosher salt

Rinse the snails well under cool, running water. Massage the grit out of the snails, being sure to get in between the foot. Drain well, and set aside in a bowl.

Place the shiitake stems and water in a medium pot. Bring to a simmer over medium heat. Reduce to 3 cups/750 ml. Strain, and reserve the mushroom broth at room temperature.

Dice the mushroom caps. In a large pot over medium heat, warm the olive oil. Sweat the onion and the garlic until translucent, about 5 minutes. Add the mushroom caps, and cook until they begin to release their liquid, about 5 minutes. Add the wine, and reduce by half. Add the reserved mushroom broth, and lower the heat to a simmer. Continue to cook until the mixture looks thick and stew-like, about 35 minutes. Stir in the Chartreuse, bring to a simmer, and remove from the heat. Add the snails, and season to taste with salt. Reserve warm for plating.

TO PLATE

Chamomile microgreens

Divide the snail ragout between 6 deep-sided bowls. Top each with a few dots of green onion purée and pickled onions. Shake the iSi canister of potato purée very well, and foam a mound to cover the ragout. Dust with the onion powder. Break off 2 large potato chips per bowl, and stand them up in the foam, tilted toward one another like a teepee. Garnish with the chamomile microgreens.

GRILLED MACKEREL, BLACK GARLIC TUILE, SMOKED-MACKEREL DASHI

We always think about presentation, but rarely does the concept for a menu item start with an actual serving piece. This grilled mackerel with smoky dashi is an exception. We have a set of beautiful, shallow, stippled beige bowls with ink-black rims, and we wanted to echo the shape and color with a black circle set in the center, which we achieve with a sweet and savory tuile made from black garlic and squid ink. The thin, round cookie is like a wide-brimmed hat, hiding the grilled fish and garnishes that lie beneath. We pour the gold dashi tableside. The plate looks so delicate, but then you crack the tuile to reveal everything below, and it turns into this briny umami bomb: the assertive oceanic flavor of the mackerel, the smoky savoriness of the dashi, sweetness from the shards of broken tuile, and funk and crunch from crosne (a member of the mint family that when fermented eats like really aggressive water chestnuts). Meyer lemon purée and fresh borage create little intermissions of floral acid and cool cucumberiness, but really this plate is all about umami. It helps us keep you on your toes in the middle of our tasting menu.

You need a smoker to make the dashi for this course (see Equipment, page xxxviii) and a grill for cooking the mackerel (on one side only, an approach I really like for the opposing textures it creates). Our "grill station" is a Japanese konro, a neat little box that sits next to the stove, topped with a wire screen and filled with glowing hunks of Pennsylvania sugar-maple charcoal, but any old backyard charcoal grill works, too. Since this recipe requires both fillets and bones, a whole fish is ideal, but if your neighborhood fish counter sells only fillets, it's worth asking if they have some heads and tails hanging around in the back. High-quality prepared fish stock is another option, in which case you could smoke the stock in a pan and then proceed to making the dashi.

MAKES 4 PORTIONS

BLACK GARLIC TUILE

3.5 ounces/100 g isomalt
3.5 ounces/100 g glucose
3.5 ounces/100 g unsalted butter
2.6 ounces/75 g black garlic
1.76 ounces/50 g all-purpose flour
1 teaspoon/4.5 g Kosher salt
1 tablespoon/15 g squid ink

Preheat the oven to 390°F. In a blender, purée the isomalt into a powder. Place the powdered isomalt and the remaining ingredients in the bowl of a stand mixer, and paddle on low speed for 2 minutes or until just combined. Spread the dough on a silicone baking mat to 1/16 inch/1.6 mm thickness. Use a 3.5-inch/85-mm circular cookie cutter to cut 4 perforated rounds into the dough. Bake the entire sheet of dough until very crisp, 7 to 10 minutes. Remove the baked dough from the tray before it is completely cooled, reserving the circular tuiles. Discard the excess. Cool the tuiles, and store them flat in a cool, dry place.

MACKEREL AND DASHI

3 ounces/85 g cherrywood chips

3 ounces/85 g applewood chips

1 whole mackerel, about 3 pounds/1.5 kg, or 4
    2-ounce/57-g fillets plus 1 pound/450 g
    mackerel bones

2.1 ounces/60 g kombu

2 quarts/2 L water, plus more for soaking woodchips

.2 ounce/5 g bonito flakes

3 ounces/85 g white soy sauce

½ teaspoon/1.5 g xanthan gum

8 ounces/240 g Kosher salt

4 ounces/114 g packed light brown sugar

Start by making the dashi. Mix the woodchips together, and soak them in enough water to cover for at least 3 hours. If you're working with a whole fish, fillet it, and reserve the fillets in the fridge. To smoke the fish bones, be sure they are very dry. Drain the woodchips. Light one large piece of lump charcoal, and let it burn until it is glowing red. Place the coal in the center of your smoker. Pile the woodchips around the coal, and let them catch fire. Once the chips are mostly burned, blow them out. Let the early smoke, which has a greenish tint, burn off. Then lay the bones over the wood, and let them smoke for 2 to 3 hours. You may need to relight the wood and then blow out the flames a few times to create continuous smoke.

Combine the smoked bones, kombu, and water in a deep pot, and bring to a simmer. Immediately remove the pot from the heat, and add the bonito. Allow to cool, and store the dashi, covered, overnight in the refrigerator.

The following day, strain the dashi through a fine sieve. Add the white soy sauce, and bring to a simmer in a large pot. Sprinkle the xanthan over the surface of the simmering dashi, and incorporate with an immersion blender for 2 minutes. Pass the dashi through a chinois into a fresh pot; it should be the consistency of heavy whipping cream. Reserve warm.

Remove the mackerel fillets from the fridge and allow them to come to room temperature. Combine the salt and brown sugar in a bowl, mix, and apply to both sides of the fillets. Cure for 20 minutes. While the fish is curing, prepare your grill. Rinse the fillets and pat dry with paper towels. Grill the mackerel, skin-side down, about 2 minutes. You want the skin very crisp, almost burnt, with the flesh mostly raw. Remove the fillets from the grill, and reserve on a plate at room temperature.

TO PLATE

Meyer Lemon Purée (see page 164)

Fermented Crosnes (see page 161)

24 Borage leaves

When the mackerel is cool enough to handle, cut each fillet into 4 equal slices and divide among 4 deep bowls. Garnish each portion of fish with 9 dots of lemon purée. Top with 6 slices of fermented crosne and 6 borage leaves. Place a tuile over each portion. Right before serving, gently pour 2 ounces of dashi around each portion.

BURNT-SUGAR SALSIFY, CURED LAMB, BLACK TRUMPETS, WATERCRESS

Four years ago we started curing our own meat. Now all of our charcuterie is done at our sister restaurant, Royal Boucherie, but when we first began curing at Laurel we only had a small refrigerator capable of curing easy cuts like lamb loin. (If you're tight on space, a wine fridge with temperature and humidity controls is perfect for making charcuterie at home.) The fat in lamb is assertive on its own. Cured, it becomes exponentially more powerful, infusing the loin with a nutty, savory flavor that makes us think of Parmigiano-Reggiano.

As a batch of lamb loins was finishing up curing (and with us not exactly sure what we would be using them for), we happened to be working on a salsify dish inspired by a method pioneered by my friend Alex Talbot. I had helped Alex out at a guest chef dinner at Elements in Princeton, New Jersey, where he served the vegetable, also known as oyster root, with vanilla ice cream, and it blew my mind. Salsify tastes like a cross between celery and artichoke, but when you cook it sous vide in caramel cut with meat stock, it takes on this wild dessert-like quality. I wanted that on the menu at Laurel, but I didn't want it in a dessert. So our play was to take a savory ingredient, manipulate it into a sweet one, then support the dish with other elements that would counteract the sweetness, which is where the cured lamb comes in. We wrap thin slices of loin around caramelized fingers of salsify, anchor that sweet-savory dynamic with earthy mushroom purée, and sharpen it with peppery watercress.

Curing the lamb at home takes between eleven and fifteen weeks, so you need to plan ahead. Although it's a time commitment, it's not an *active* time commitment. The loins do their thing and require minimal maintenance. Look for meat from domestic lambs, which are bigger and thus better for curing.

MAKES 4 PORTIONS

CURED LAMB

1 lamb loin, 1 to 2 pounds/453 to 907 g, with fat cap
Kosher salt
2 cups/454 ml Chablis
2 tablespoons/6 g chopped rosemary
1 tablespoon/1.5 g toasted and chopped fennel seed

Weigh the lamb loin. Calculate 3.8 percent of the weight, and measure that out in salt. Divide the salt in half. Season the lamb loin with half the salt, wrap it tightly in a single layer of cheesecloth, place it in a nonreactive airtight container, and refrigerate for 10 days. After 10 days, unwrap the lamb, rinse well, and pat dry. Season with the remaining salt. Rewrap it tightly in fresh cheesecloth, and refrigerate it for another 11 days. After 11 days, unwrap the lamb and rinse it with the Chablis. Rub the lamb with the rosemary and fennel seed. Wrap it tightly in cheesecloth, and hang it in a temperature- and humidity-controlled space at 58°F with 60 percent humidity. Leave it to dry for 2 to 3 months, until the loin has lost 25 to 30 percent of its weight and feels firm to the touch.

WATERCRESS PURÉE

2 quarts/2 L water
½ cup/150 g Kosher salt, plus more as needed
8 ounces/227 g stemmed watercress leaves
½ teaspoon/2 g xanthan gum

Boil the water and add the salt. Blanch the watercress leaves in the water for 3 minutes and 30 seconds. Strain the watercress, and shock it in ice water. Strain again. Squeeze out the excess liquid, and purée the watercress in a blender with the xanthan gum. Season to taste with salt, and reserve the purée in a plastic squeeze bottle for serving.

WATERCRESS OIL

1 pound/454 g stemmed watercress leaves
4 ounces/120 g grapeseed oil

Combine the watercress leaves and oil in a blender, and purée on high. Transfer the purée to a sauce-pot, bring to a simmer, and remove from the heat. Strain the purée through a chinois into a metal bowl, and immediately cool over ice. Transfer to a plastic squeeze bottle for serving.

BLACK TRUMPET MUSHROOM PURÉE

1 shallot, brunoised
2 tablespoons/30 g unsalted butter, divided
1 pound black trumpet mushrooms
½ cup/120 g Madeira
1 cup/240 g Roasted Chicken Stock (see page 156)

Sauté the shallot in 1 tablespoon butter in a medium pot over medium heat until golden-brown, about 3 minutes. Add the mushrooms, sweat for 2 minutes, and deglaze the pot with Madeira. Add the chicken stock, and simmer for 10 minutes until the mushrooms are tender. Transfer the mixture to a blender and purée until smooth. Return the puree to the pot and whisk in the remaining butter. Reserve warm.

BURNT-SUGAR SALSIFY

Juice of 1 lemon
2 quarts/2 L water
4 pieces salsify, about 3 ounces/85 g each
1 cup/225 g granulated sugar
2 cups/480 ml Lamb Stock (see page 155)

Add the lemon juice to the water. Peel and cut each piece of salsify into 4 2.5-inch/6-cm pieces, for a total of 16 pieces. Place the cut salsify in the acidulated water.

Set a circulator to 185°F. Cook the sugar in a saucepan over high heat until very dark brown and almost smoking, about 5 minutes. Deglaze with the lamb stock, remove from heat, and allow the mixture to cool to room temperature. Transfer the salsify with about 1 cup/240 ml of the burnt-sugar mixture to a large vacuum bag and seal on high. Reserve the remaining mixture. Cook the salsify sous vide for 45 minutes. Remove the salsify from the bag for plating, and strain the liquid into a saucepot with the remaining mixture. Cook the liquid over medium heat until it has reduced into a slightly thickened, shiny jus. Reserve warm.

TO PLATE

12 nasturtium leaves
Fermented Black Trumpet Mushroom Powder (see page 162)

Slice 16 pieces of cured lamb as thinly as possible on a meat slicer or with a very sharp knife. Wrap each piece of salsify with 1 slice of cured lamb. Spoon 2 tablespoons/30 g of black trumpet purée onto a large plate, and arrange 4 pieces of wrapped salsify on top. Squeeze 1 small dot of watercress purée onto each piece of salsify. Garnish with 3 nasturtium leaves. Dust the plate with black trumpet powder. Add the watercress oil to the reserved lamb jus, and stir to combine. Spoon 1 tablespoon of the jus-oil mix alongside the salsify, where it will begin to separate into brown and green sauces. Repeat for remaining portions.

DUCK BREAST, CARAMELIZED SUNCHOKE, BLACKBERRY, CHICORY

You can be inspired by the classics and still expand on them. That's what happens in this course, where modern plating visually recasts a pairing that has been around for centuries: game with berries. A duck plate wouldn't have looked this way at Le Bec-Fin (and the duck wouldn't have been cooked sous vide in chicory-infused duck fat), but we often paired lightly gamy meats with meat sauces that had been fortified by some type of berry preserve. Here, we update that combination with additions of bittersweet cocoa and coffee notes (in the duck fat and in the crumble) and with caramelized sunchoke purée, which is based on a visit I made to the headquarters of *Modernist Cuisine* in Seattle. They make a caramelized-carrot soup by pressure-cooking carrots with baking soda, which changes the pH and lets the vegetables pick up caramelization much more rapidly than they would in a regular pan. We take that principle and apply it to sunchokes, which bring an earthy sweetness to the plate.

CURED DUCK BREAST

1 duck breast, about 8 ounces/240 g
1.5 ounces/43 g Kosher salt
1 tablespoon/3 g juniper berries
1 tablespoon/14 g packed light brown sugar
1 tablespoon/1 g rosemary leaves

Make the cure by combining the salt, juniper berries, brown sugar, and rosemary. Divide the cure in half. Rub the duck with half of the cure. Wrap the duck in plastic, and refrigerate for 5 days. Remove, unwrap, and rinse the duck. Pat dry. Apply the remaining cure. Wrap the duck in plastic and refrigerate for 6 days. Remove, unwrap, and rinse the duck. Pat dry, and insert an S-hook through the tail end of the breast. Hang in a temperature- and humidity-controlled space at 58°F with 60 percent humidity for 2 to 4 weeks, until the meat is dark and very firm. Wrap in plastic and reserve cold.

CARAMELIZED SUNCHOKE PURÉE

2.7 pounds/1,200 g sunchokes, cut in 1.5-inch/4-cm pieces
7 ounces/200 g heavy whipping cream
7 ounces/200 g whole milk
1 teaspoon/3 g baking soda

Place all the ingredients in the bowl of a stovetop pressure cooker. Bring to a gentle simmer, and simmer for 10 minutes. Lock the pressure cooker, and cook on medium pressure for 18 minutes. Remove from the heat, and let the pressure release naturally, about 15 minutes. Make sure all steam has been released before removing the lid. Strain off the liquid, and purée the sunchokes until very smooth. Pass through a chinois, and reserve warm.

CHICORY CRUMBLE

3.5 ounces/100 g cocoa powder
3.5 ounces/100 g all-purpose flour
7 ounces/200 g granulated sugar
1.4 ounces/40 g chicory powder
.2 ounce/5 g Kosher salt
1.8 ounces/50 g unsalted butter, melted

Preheat the oven to 325°F. Stir all the dry ingredients together in a bowl. Drizzle the butter over the top, and mix together using your hands. The mixture should come together if squeezed but fall apart when disturbed. Spread the dough evenly on a half sheet pan, and bake for 8 to 12 minutes or until crisp. Remove the crumble from the oven. When it's cool enough to handle, break it apart into small pieces—it should look like soil. Reserve at room temperature.

DUCK BREASTS

8 ounces/228 g duck fat
1 ounce/28 g dried chicory powder
2 8-ounce/228-g duck breasts, brined for 12 hours in
Duck Brine (see page 158) and patted dry

Set a circulator to 135°F. Warm the duck fat in a saucepan to 140°F. Stir the chicory powder into the fat, steep for 7 minutes off the heat, and strain into a large vacuum bag. Place the brined duck breasts in the bag with the chicory-infused duck fat, and seal on high. Place the bag in the water bath and lower the temperature to 129°F. Cook for 2 hours and 15 minutes. Remove from the water bath, and let the duck cool at room temperature for 20 minutes.

After the duck has cooled for 20 minutes, preheat a large cast-iron skillet on the stove over medium heat. Let the duck breasts cool for an additional 10 minutes, then add them to the pan skin-side down; they should sizzle when they hit the pan. Cook the breasts until the fat has been rendered and the skin is crisp, about 3 minutes. Baste the flesh side of the breast with the rendered duck fat. Remove the duck from the heat, and let stand at room temperature for 5 minutes before plating.

TO PLATE

1 cup/250 g Duck Jus (see page 156)
4 blackberries
1 tablespoon/15ml blackberry vinegar
12 jasmine blossoms

Slice the cured duck breast into 8 pieces as thinly as possible on a meat slicer or with a very sharp knife. Warm the jus over low heat. Trim the ends off the blackberries, then cut each berry crosswise into 4 equal slices. Marinate the blackberry slices for a few minutes in a small bowl with the blackberry vinegar. Trim the ends and sides off each duck breast to create an even 4-inch/10-cm rectangle, then cut each rectangle in half lengthwise. Each slice will be about 1 inch/2.5 cm thick. Place a piece of the duck breast on a large plate, cut-side up and skin facing sideways. Spoon 1 tablespoon/15 g sunchoke purée onto the plate, and cover half the purée with 1 tablespoon/10 g chicory crumble. Garnish around the plate with 4 marinated blackberry slices, a quarter of the remaining vinegar, 2 slices of cured duck, 1 tablespoon/15 g duck jus, and 3 jasmine blossoms. Repeat for the remaining portions.

ROASTED APPLE, CARAMEL-COFFEE CREAM, BLACK WALNUT, APPLE WINE

There's not exactly a lot of fruit growing in the Delaware Valley in late fall, but that's fine with me. This dessert goes back to my love for apples. As a kid, picking them was a family tradition; as a teenager, the tradition became riding dirt bikes through the orchards with my brothers and friends. This dish also brings the fall menu full circle. We begin with Granny Smith. We end with Stayman Winesap, a crisp heirloom with a balanced sweet-tart profile. We bake them whole at a low temperature for 36 hours, during which time they slowly turn into what look like apple artifacts. Underneath the oven-wrinkled skin, the flesh is soft enough to cut with a spoon, and the flavor is a powerful concentration of sweetness and acid. We core the apples, then fill the cavities with coffee pastry cream and pâte de fruit made with apple wine from William Heritage Winery in South Jersey; my chef de cuisine, Eddie, is a friend of the winemaker. Apple vinegar gel and a flurry of caramel black walnut powder show up to finish, so in each bite you get stewed sweetness, sparkling acid, rich fat, and bitterness.

Unlike with other dry ingredients, you can't just grind nuts into a powder because of their oil content. If we didn't use liquid nitrogen here, we'd wind up with black walnut butter. The nitro flash-freezes the nuts, suspending their fats in a solid form and thus making them powderable. If you can't get your hands on liquid nitrogen, mince the walnuts as finely as you can, and mix them together with the caramel powder. You won't get the exact same textural effect, but the flavor will be very close.

This recipe makes six apples, but you'll have enough coffee-caramel cream (and certainly enough of the other elements) to increase the number of servings to ten or twelve apples if you're inclined to invite more people over. Or pipe the extra cream into tarte shells and dust them with the leftover walnut powder for an easy and impressive weekday dessert.

ROASTED APPLES

6 Stayman Winesap apples

Preheat the oven to 175°F. Wash the apples well and place them stem up on a sheet pan lined with a silicone baking mat. Bake the apples for 36 hours, after which they will look slightly wrinkled and have a brown tint. Let the apples cool on the tray. Once they are cool enough to handle, turn an apple upside-down and remove the core with a paring knife. Do not cut all the way through the apple; the stem should remain intact. You want to cut a hole that's about ¾ inch/2 cm in diameter. Repeat for remaining apples. Reserve cold until serving.

CARAMEL-COFFEE CREAM

1.3 ounces/35 g glucose syrup
3.5 ounces/100 g granulated sugar, divided
6 ounces/170 g heavy whipping cream, divided
11 ounces/308 g unsalted butter, cubed, divided
1.75 ounces/50 g whole milk
3 egg yolks
1 teaspoon/5 g coffee extract

Combine glucose and half the sugar in a small, heavy-bottomed pot. Heat over medium heat until the sugar melts, starts to bubble, and turns caramel in color, about 5 minutes. Add 3.4 ounces/95 g of the heavy whipping cream to the pot and whisk vigorously, being sure to release any bits stuck to the bottom. Add .3 ounce/8 g of the butter, and return the blend to a boil, mixing well. Set aside.

In a separate pot, bring the milk to a simmer. Meanwhile, in a mixing bowl, whisk together the remaining sugar and the egg yolks. Once the milk is simmering, slowly pour it into the egg mixture, whisking constantly. Set the mixture over a double boiler, and whisk until it becomes thick. Remove the bowl from the heat and whisk in the remaining 10.7 ounces/300 g butter, the reserved caramel, and the coffee extract. Let the mixture cool in the bowl.

Whip the remaining 2.6 ounces/75 g heavy whipping cream to stiff peaks. Fold the whipped cream gently into the caramel-coffee cream, and transfer it to a piping bag. Reserve cold.

APPLE WINE PÂTE DE FRUIT

14 ounces/420 g water, divided
.25 ounce/10 g tartaric acid
15.2 ounces/430 g granulated sugar, divided
.25 ounce/10 g pectin
7 ounces/200 g apple wine
Cooking spray, for greasing
1 cup/225 g sanding sugar

In a small bowl, mix .75 ounce/20 g of the water with the tartaric acid and set aside. In another small bowl, mix 1 ounce/30 g of the granulated sugar with the pectin and set aside. Combine 13.3 ounces/400 g of water and the apple wine in a medium pot, and whisk in the pectin-sugar mixture. Boil it for 60 seconds. Add the remaining 14.2 ounces/400 g of granulated sugar to the pot, and return the mixture to a boil. Cook until it registers 230°F on a candy thermometer, and add the tartaric acid solution. Lightly grease a shallow pan measuring about 13 x 7 inches/33 x 18 cm with cooking spray. Pour the mixture into the pan, and let it set for 3 hours in the fridge. Cut the pâte de fruit into rounds that are slightly smaller in diameter than the diameter of the apples' holes. Dust them with sanding sugar, and reserve at room temperature.

BLACK WALNUT CARAMEL POWDER

3.5 ounces/100 g granulated sugar
3.5 ounces/100 g glucose syrup
4.6 ounces/140 g heavy whipping cream
1 ounce/30 g unsalted butter
.6 ounce/18 g tapioca maltodextrin
3.5 ounces/100 g black walnut meats
Liquid nitrogen
1 teaspoon/5 g Kosher salt

Preheat the oven to 325°F. Combine the sugar and the glucose in a small, heavy-bottomed pot. Bring the mixture to 235°F on a candy thermometer. Add the cream, and return the mixture to a boil. Remove from the heat, and stir in the butter. Pour the caramel onto a sheet tray lined with a silicone baking mat, and let it cool to room temperature. When it's cool enough to handle, break the hardened caramel into small pieces; place them in the bowl of a food processor with the tapioca maltodextrin. Process until powdered; set aside. Meanwhile, toast the black walnuts in the oven for 10 minutes or until golden-brown. Cool the nuts to room temperature, and transfer them to a blender. Carefully add enough liquid nitrogen to cover the nuts, and purée until you achieve a fine, fluffy powder. Mix the walnut powder with the caramel powder and the salt. Reserve in a bowl.

APPLE VINEGAR GEL

8.8 ounces/235 g apple vinegar
1 tablespoon/10 g granulated sugar
1 teaspoon/2.8 g agar-agar

Purée all the ingredients together in a blender. Transfer the mixture to a small pot, and bring it to a simmer, whisking continuously. Simmer for 2 minutes. Remove from the heat, and cool the mix in the pot until it's completely gelled. Return the gel to the blender, purée, and pass through a chinois into a plastic squeeze bottle for serving.

TO PLATE

Preheat the oven to 250°F. Warm the apples in the oven until the interior of an apple registers 125°F on an instant-read thermometer. Set an apple upside down on a cutting board. Place a pâte de fruit in the apple's cavity. Fill the cavity with coffee cream, and cap it with another pâte de fruit. Repeat for the remaining apples. Turn the apples upright, and set each one in the center of a plate. Spoon a generous amount of the walnut caramel powder over each apple, and garnish each plate with 3 dots of apple vinegar gel.

COCKTAIL: DRUNKEN FARMER

Like fat purple teardrops, figs drip from century-old trees all over the city and suburbs in mid to late September, including one at my in-laws' house. The fruits are what everyone waits all summer for, but I've taken to harvesting the leaves ever since Ian Brendle, the ninth-generation farmer at Green Meadow Farm in Lancaster County, suggested steeping them in hot simple syrup. The result tastes just like coconut. We strain the fig leaf syrup and shake it with lime, bourbon (we recommend Four Roses here), and egg white, then top it with a few drops of house-made fennel cordial. You need very little of the cordial to make this cocktail; it's there more for aroma than taste, cancelling out any lingering egg smell, but the batch will keep about 2 months at room temperature. For a farmer on the fly, substitute Don Ciccio & Figli Finocchietto fennel liqueur.

MAKES 1 COCKTAIL

FENNEL CORDIAL

1 ounce/30 g dried fennel blossoms
1 quart/1 L vodka

Combine the fennel and vodka in a bottle. Let it mature in a cool, dry place for about 3 weeks, checking the flavor every other day. Once the fennel overtakes the vodka smell and flavor, strain, rebottle, and reserve. It lasts for about 2 months.

FIG LEAF SYRUP

18 ounces/500 g granulated sugar
2 cups/500 g water
3 large fig leaves

Combine the sugar with the water in a saucepot over medium heat. Bring to a simmer, stirring to dissolve the sugar. Add the fig leaves, and simmer for 10 minutes. Strain, discard the leaves, and cool the syrup. Transfer to a plastic squeeze bottle and reserve cold.

TO SERVE

1.5 ounces/45 ml bourbon
.75 ounce/23 ml lime juice
.75 ounce/23 ml Fig Leaf Syrup
.5 ounce/15 g egg white
½ cup ice
Fennel Cordial, for serving

Combine the bourbon, lime juice, fig leaf syrup, and egg white in a shaker, and dry shake until frothy. Add the ice, and shake for 20 to 25 seconds. Strain into a coupe glass. Once the egg white foam has settled on the surface, about 10 seconds, add 4 drops of fennel cordial, using an eyedropper.

Tonight We Are Serving

I.
Frozen Beet, Sumac, Pomegranate

II.
Kasu-Cured Fluke, Citrus, Olive Oil

III.
Warm Truffle Custard, Surf Clam, Makrut Lime

IV.
Pan-Roasted Halibut Cheek,
White Asparagus, Quince Confit

V.
Bourbon-Glazed Grilled Lobster,
Crunchy Grains, Apple Blossom

VI.
Fresh Ricotta Gnocchi, Black Truffle, Toasted Sourdough

VII.
Black Trumpet Mushroom–Stuffed Dover Sole,
Chicken Jus, Whey Onions

VIII.
Hay-Cured Squab en Vessie

IX.
Yuzu Curd, Black Sesame, Torched Malt Crisp

X.
Cocktail: The Kali

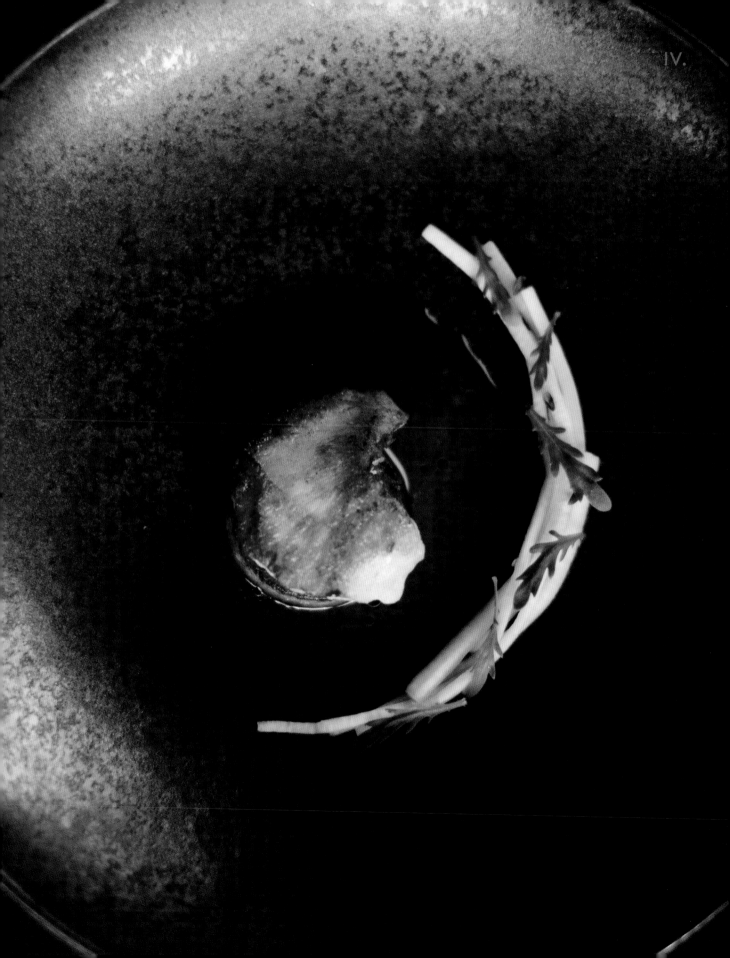

IX.

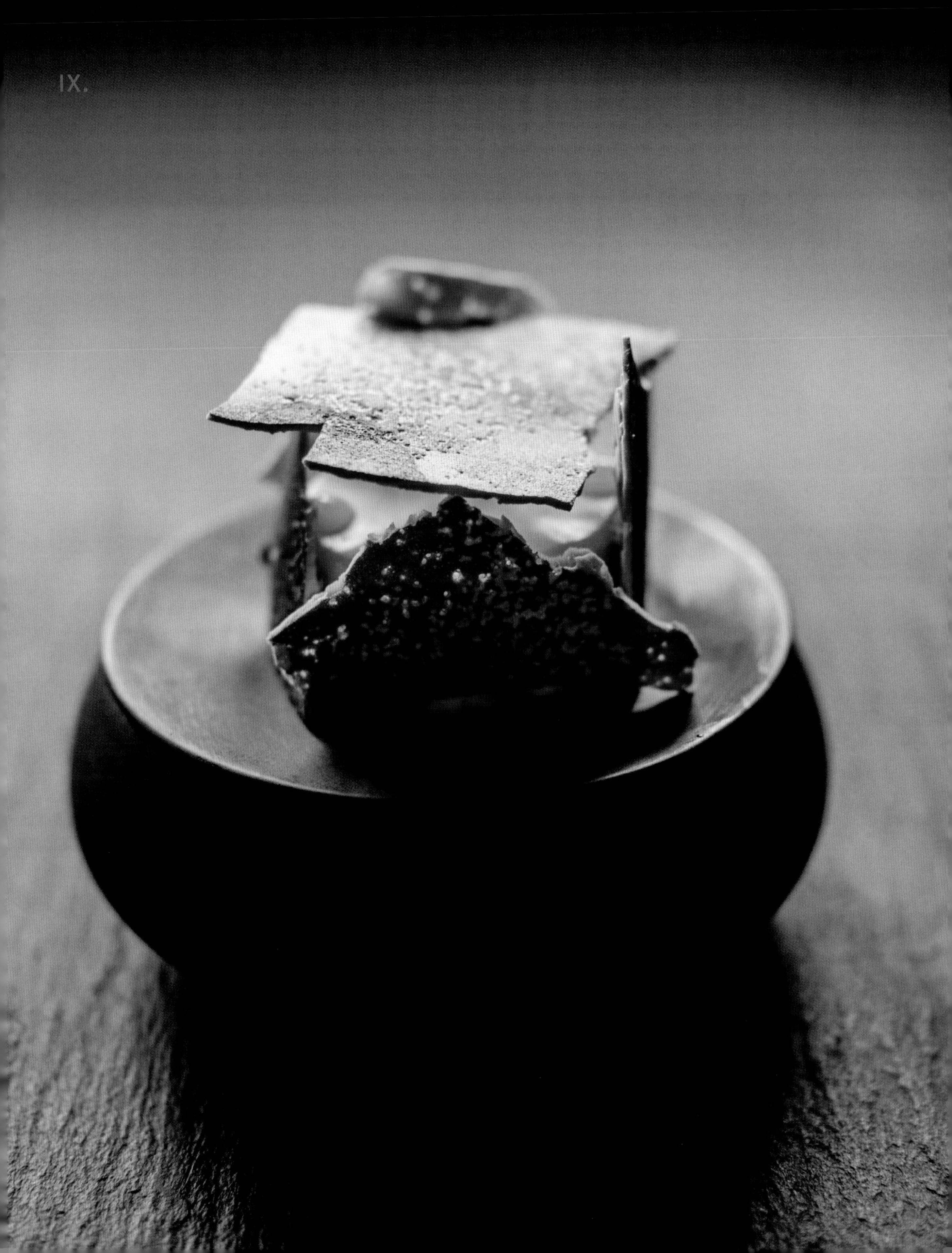

FROZEN BEET, SUMAC, POMEGRANATE

Winter food is warming, hearty, nourishing. But as a restaurant that's not serving lasagna, chicken pot pie, and brownie sundaes (wherever that is—and please take me there), we need to think about how we can hit those sensations in ways our guests don't necessarily expect. Something frozen, for example. Doesn't sound very wintry, but when the frozen something in question is a beet mousse, that deeply savory background note has no trouble standing up to the temperature. Beets are also perfect vehicles for acid and sweetness, two flavors we always try to achieve in an opening course. Pomegranate (in the mousse and as a gel) and sumac dusted over the top play those supporting roles, so you get a profound earthiness when you pop the frozen mousse in your mouth, then, as it disappears, a bright finish.

We use Versawhip to build volume in this mousse. It takes the place of egg whites (this snack happens to be vegan) and creates a more stable structure that holds its shape after being piped out and plunged into liquid nitrogen. We use nitro twice in this recipe, both to freeze the mousse and to make the powdered sumac (same as with the black walnuts in our Roasted Apples, page 38). If you can't get liquid nitrogen, pipe out the beet mousse on a parchment-lined sheet tray, and freeze until set. You can also substitute ground sumac for fresh, though the flower's lemony quality won't be nearly as intense.

Final note: this recipe has the highest yield you'll find in the book, and that's not because we didn't want to scale it down to a neat number of portions. If you try making the mousse in a smaller batch, it won't hold its shape. The total quantity is actually not that much; the one-bite size inflates the yield, so feel free to experiment with freezing larger portions.

BEET MOUSSE AND BEET-SUMAC POWDER

3 pounds/1.4 kg red beets
.4 ounce/12 g Kosher salt, divided
4 cones fresh sumac
Liquid nitrogen
½ cup/115 g pomegranate juice
3 ounces/85.1 g granulated sugar
½ teaspoon/2.5 g xanthan gum
2 tablespoons/12.5 g Versawhip

Juice the beets, reserving the pulp in the juicer. Strain the juice through a chinois 3 times, reserving the pulp. Weigh out 12 ounces/340 g of beet juice, and freeze it in a nonreactive airtight container.

Combine the reserved beet pulp from the juicer and the chinois with .3 ounce/9 g of the salt in a large vacuum bag. Seal on high, and leave at room temperature for 4 days or until the bag puffs. Strain off and discard the liquid. Dehydrate the pulp at 110°F for 2 days or until hard. Powder it in a spice grinder.

Remove the sumac blossoms from each cone, and place them in a blender. Pour enough liquid nitrogen over the blossoms to cover, and let them freeze for 1 minute. Blend at medium speed to grind the sumac into a powder. Combine the sumac and the beet powders together, and reserve in a mesh-top shaker.

Defrost the beet juice. Add the pomegranate juice, sugar, and remaining salt. Mix well to dissolve the sugar, and strain the mixture through a chinois. Place the liquid in a blender. Purée on low for 30 seconds, add the xanthan, and purée for 2 more minutes. Add the Versawhip, and purée for 2 minutes. Transfer 16 ounces/500 g of the liquid to a stand mixer fitted with a whisk attachment. Whip on medium-high speed for 5 to 10 minutes, until the purée has the

texture of shaving cream. Transfer the mousse to a piping bag. Reserve cold.

POMEGRANATE GEL

17.6 ounces/500 g pomegranate juice
.4 ounce/12 g sherry vinegar
.2 ounce/6 g granulated sugar
.2 ounce/5.2 g agar-agar

Combine the juice, vinegar, and sugar in a blender, and purée. Sprinkle in the agar, and purée on low for 2 minutes. Transfer the blend to a small pot, and slowly bring it to a simmer, whisking continuously. Remove from the heat, and pour the mixture into a shallow pan. Let the gel set until firm and cool. Purée in a blender, pass through a chinois, and reserve in a plastic squeeze bottle for plating.

TO PLATE

Liquid nitrogen

Set a large stainless-steel bowl on a dish towel. Wearing gloves, fill the bowl halfway with liquid nitrogen. Pipe a golf ball–sized dome of beet mousse onto a small square of waxed paper. Top with 1 dot of pomegranate gel. Carefully place the paper upside down in the bowl, and remove the paper. Once the mousse is frozen, remove it from the nitrogen and place it on a serving spoon. Dust with sumac-beet powder. Allow it to rest for 15 seconds, then serve. Repeat for remaining portions.

KASU-CURED FLUKE, CITRUS, OLIVE OIL

Hidden layers of flavor are the difference between food that tastes good, food that tastes great, and food that tastes spectacular. We're always mindful of this fact when developing dishes. These layers turn up both in raw ingredients, like green farro, which has a smoky, green-tea quality from the fire-threshing process it undergoes during harvest, and in ones we manipulate behind the scenes. Take this fluke. You can't *see* the kasu cure we apply. You may not even be able to pinpoint the subtle fermented-rice flavor. But remove the kasu from the dish, and it'll taste like something is missing. Scott Anderson at Elements was the first chef to serve me fish cured with kasu, the miso-like byproduct of sake production. I love sake. The breadth of varieties in the category is stunning. Scott's warm kasu trout was a wow moment, and I was excited to try it out at Laurel with fluke, a perfect fish for curing, in an early course with lots of different citrus elements. I've learned over the years that if you combine equal parts of different citruses—say lemon, lime, and grapefruit juices—the mix doesn't taste like any of those fruits. It just reads as . . . citrus, and it unfolds with unbelievable layers of brightness. Here, that sleight-of-hand is at play with Buddha's hand, Meyer lemon, calamansi, yuzu, and kumquats. Have I mentioned that I'm an acid freak? Citrus peaks in the winter, and I'm here for it. A note on fluke: We like to use fish that are in the five- to six-pound range. The fillets are thick enough without being tough, and the fish has lived long enough to develop good flavor.

MAKES 4 PORTIONS

KUMQUAT UMEBOSHI

1 pound/454 g kumquats
1 quart/1 L vodka
8.8 ounces/250 g green shiso leaves
2 ounces/57 g coarse sea salt

Rinse the kumquats very well, checking for blemishes or imperfections. Any damaged fruit can ruin the entire batch. Soak the kumquats in the vodka for 12 hours. Remove the kumquats from the vodka, and let them air dry. Rub some vodka in a 6 x 6-inch/15 x 15-cm curing container. Place a layer of shiso at the bottom of the container, followed by some salt, a layer of kumquats, more salt, and then start over with the shiso again. Repeat the layering process until all the kumquats are covered in salt and shiso. Weigh down the kumquats with an 8-ounce/227-g weight. Cover the container with a piece of cheesecloth secured with a rubber band. Leave it in a cool, dry place for 1 week or until the kumquats have released enough liquid for them to be completely covered. Remove the fruit from the brine. Discard the brine, and dry the kumquats for 3 hours in a dehydrator set to 110°F. Store them in a nonreactive airtight container in the refrigerator.

CURED FLUKE

8 ounces/227 g kasu
3 ounces/85.1 g Kosher salt
4 ounces/113.4 g water
1 skinned fluke fillet, about 8 ounces/227 g

Place the kasu and the salt in the bowl of a food processor. Turn it on, and slowly pour the water in to emulsify the ingredients and make the cure. Rub the cure on both sides of the fluke fillet, and wrap the fish in plastic. Refrigerate for 2 hours. Rinse the fluke, and pat dry with paper towels. Reserve it in the refrigerator for plating.

BUDDHA'S HAND CONFIT

1 large Buddha's hand
2 quarts/2 L plus 3 ounces/85 g water, divided
1 cup/225 g granulated sugar
2 ounces/57 g yuzu juice
Juice of half a lemon

Slice the fingers off the Buddha's hand and wash them. Slice them on a mandoline to ¹⁄₁₆–¹⁄₈ inch/.2–.3 cm thick. Bring 2 quarts/2 L of water to a boil. Blanch the Buddha's hand slices for 15 seconds, then shock them in ice water. In a small pot combine the sugar, yuzu juice, lemon juice, and 3 ounces/85.1 g water. Bring to a simmer to dissolve the sugar, then cool. Divide the Buddha's hand slices between 3 small vacuum bags. Pour 4 ounces of the cooled liquid into each bag. Seal on high. Open each bag and seal on high twice more. Reserve cold in the bags.

CALAMANSI BROTH

3.5 ounces/100 g calamansi juice
.4 ounce/12.5 g granulated sugar
1.25 ounces/35.4 g Kosher salt
Pinch MSG
8 ounces/225 g water
1½ teaspoons/.4 g xanthan gum

Combine the calamansi juice, sugar, salt, MSG, and water in a blender. Purée until smooth. Add the xanthan, and purée again for 2 minutes. Strain into a nonreactive container and reserve cold.

TO PLATE

Olio Verde
Maldon salt
Meyer Lemon Purée (see page 164)
20 mizuna flowers

Slice 20 thin slices of kumquat umeboshi. Remove the fluke from the fridge. Slice it ¹⁄₁₆ inch/1.6 mm thick, and divide into 4 equal portions. Rub the fluke with Olio Verde and Maldon salt. Place 1 portion of the fluke in a shallow bowl. Garnish with 3 dots of lemon purée, 5 slices of Buddha's hand, 5 slices of kumquat umeboshi, and 5 flowers. Spoon 2 ounces/56 g calamansi broth around the fish. Repeat for remaining portions.

WARM TRUFFLE CUSTARD, SURF CLAM, MAKRUT LIME

I grew up on the New Hampshire coast eating steamers and chowder clams and oysters as big as the palm of my hand at Brown's, an old-school place in Seabrook with one line for lobsters, another for clams, and a third for fried stuff. This was my family's gathering place. When I brought my wife to meet my parents for the first time, we went to Brown's. So seafood is very much a part of who I am and how I grew up. In Philly, we're less than sixty miles from the ocean, and we get absolutely outstanding clams in the winter. They're featured here with a warm truffle custard, a balance of salty and earthy accented with a flash of aromatic makrut lime zest and lacto-fermented daylilies that have been hanging out in our fermentation cave (aka basement) from the previous spring. We call for surf clam here, but a meaty chowder clam (quahog) also works great. Be sure to save and clean the shells after shucking. They make a beautiful presentation when you bake the custards in them, or you can substitute crème brûlée dishes.

MAKES 4 PORTIONS

TRUFFLE VINAIGRETTE

2 shallots, brunoised
½ cup/110 g truffle jus
½ cup/110 g Banyuls vinegar
2.1 ounces/60 g granulated sugar
1.1 ounces/30 g grated black truffle
1½ tablespoons/20 g extra-virgin olive oil

Combine the shallots, truffle jus, vinegar, and sugar in a small pot. Reduce the contents over medium-high heat by two-thirds; remove from the heat. Add the grated truffle and cover. Steep for 20 minutes, then cool completely. Whisk in the olive oil and reserve warm.

TRUFFLE CUSTARD

½ cup/100 g truffle jus
1.75 ounces/50 g grated black truffle
3 eggs
1 cup/240 g whole milk
1 cup/240 g heavy whipping cream
1 teaspoon/5 g Kosher salt
2 surf clams, about 9 ounces/270g each
1.5 quarts/1.4 L hot water

Preheat the oven to 220°F. Combine the truffle jus, grated truffle, and eggs in a blender, and purée until smooth. In a small saucepan, combine the milk and cream, and bring to a simmer. With the blender running on low, slowly pour the warm liquid into the blender until the ingredients are completely combined. Add the salt, purée to combine, and reserve the mixture warm.

Gently shuck the clams, and wash the 4 shells very well. Reserve 1 clam for another use. Pull out the adductors of the second clam, and cut away the tongue (or foot). Plunge the adductors and tongue into ice water, and gently massage them to remove any sand. Remove the clam from the water and pat it dry with paper towels. Thinly slice the tongue of the clam, and cut the adductors into small wedges. Reserve chilled until serving.

Divide the custard base among the 4 clam shells, but do not overfill. There will be some left over. Place a dish towel in a 21 x 13-inch/53 x 33-cm pan, and carefully arrange the filled shells on top of the towel. Pour the hot water into the pan to a depth of halfway up the shells. Cover the pan with foil, and bake for 20 minutes or until the custard is set.

TO PLATE

Borage flowers
Thyme flowers
Fermented Daylilies (see page 161)
Grated zest of 1 makrut lime

Divide the pieces of clam among the 4 custards, arranging them in a ring around the surface of each. Garnish each custard with the flowers and a few slices of fermented daylily. Spoon the vinaigrette into the empty spaces between the clams. Garnish with the lime zest.

PAN-ROASTED HALIBUT CHEEK, WHITE ASPARAGUS, QUINCE CONFIT

We first developed this dish in 2015 as we were transitioning Laurel from an à la carte menu to the tasting-menu format we use now. The tasting menu's original price was $75 for seven courses, which meant we had to work with cost-effective ingredients and transform them into something spectacular. Halibut cheeks were one of those ingredients. Our fish guy dropped some off to us one day, and I fell in love with the texture they take on when you cook them gently, how they flake apart into segmented striations—like skate wing but better. Even though halibut cheeks have gotten trendy and have more than doubled in price, we still love them and use them in our late-winter menus.

Pacific halibut season opens in March, about the same time as the first spears of white asparagus are ready for harvest in Norway. While we pride ourselves on working with Mid-Atlantic produce, there are some things other countries just do best. White asparagus is one of them. It's grown by forcing: the spears are continually covered in soil as they sprout. Because chlorophyll never has a chance to develop, the asparagus lacks not only the usual green color but also the grassy flavor. Instead, you have something sweet and bright and stark white. In this dish, we feature two preparations of white asparagus—quickly cured and fermented for eight days—for two different expressions of the same flavor. Look to specialty produce markets for sourcing fresh white asparagus. There are some high-quality jarred versions, but the preserved stuff won't work in this recipe. If you can't find white asparagus, use green.

MAKES 4 PORTIONS

ASPARAGUS JUS

**2 pounds/900 g white asparagus, cut in
 1-inch/2.5-cm slices and divided**
.5 ounce/13.5 g Kosher salt
1½ teaspoons/4 g xanthan gum
Juice of half a lime
1 tablespoon/15 g white soy sauce

Reserve half the asparagus cold. Pulse the remaining asparagus with the salt in a food processor until it becomes a paste. Use a spatula to scrape the asparagus into a small vacuum bag, and seal on high. Leave the bag out at room temperature in a cool, dry place for 4 days or until the bag puffs. Open the bag, strain out the liquid, and discard the solids. Purée the asparagus liquid and the reserved cold asparagus in the food processor. Transfer the purée to a fresh vacuum bag, and seal on high. Leave the bag out at room temperature in a cool, dry place for 4 days or until the bag puffs. Open the bag, strain the liquid into a blender, and discard the solids. Add the xanthan gum to the blender, and purée until smooth. Season with the lime juice and the white soy sauce, and strain through a chinois. Reserve the liquid in the refrigerator.

CURED ASPARAGUS

3 jumbo white asparagus
Kosher salt

Cut the asparagus into batons that are 5 inches/13 cm long and .25 inch/.6 cm thick. Weigh the batons, and calculate 2.5 percent of the weight in salt. Season the asparagus with the salt, and let it sit at room temperature for 6 hours or until pliable. Rinse and reserve cold.

QUINCE CONFIT

1 large quince
1 teaspoon/5 g Kosher salt
1 teaspoon/5 g granulated sugar
2 tablespoons/30 g extra-virgin olive oil
1 small sprig white spruce (substitute rosemary)
1 sprig thyme

Set a circulator to 185°F. Rinse the quince to remove the outer fuzz. Working quickly, peel the quince, cut it into slices ½ inch/1 cm thick, and punch out 4 coins with a 1.5-inch/4-cm cookie cutter. Season the quince slices with the salt and sugar. Place them in a small vacuum bag with the olive oil, spruce, and thyme. Seal on high. Cook sous vide for 30 minutes. Reserve in the bag at room temperature.

HALIBUT CHEEKS

1 cup/225 g Kosher salt
½ cup/113 g packed dark brown sugar
4 cleaned halibut cheeks, 1.5 to 2 ounces/43 to 57 g each
1 tablespoon/15 g unsalted butter

Preheat the oven to 300°F. Mix the salt and sugar together in a bowl until combined. Heavily season the cheeks on each side, and set aside for 10 minutes in the fridge. Rinse the fish well and pat dry with paper towels.

Brown the butter in a small sauté pan and add the halibut cheeks. Lightly pan-fry them over medium-high heat for about 2 minutes per side. Transfer the cheeks to a small pan, and finish them in the oven until warmed through, about 4 minutes. Remove from the oven.

TO PLATE

1 tablespoon/15 g unsalted butter
20 thyme leaves
20 chrysanthemum sprouts
Kale Oil (see page 163)

Melt the butter in a sauté pan, and sauté the 4 coins of quince on one side only. Divide the quince coins between 4 serving bowls, and top each with a halibut cheek. Arrange a small bunch of asparagus batons in a half-moon around each portion of quince and halibut. Garnish each bundle of asparagus with 5 thyme leaves and 5 chrysanthemum sprouts. Whisk together ½ cup/113 g of asparagus jus and ¼ cup/60 g of kale oil in a small bowl, and spoon the blend around each cheek.

BOURBON-GLAZED GRILLED LOBSTER, CRUNCHY GRAINS, APPLE BLOSSOMS

In a way, I have to thank Chef Perrier for this dish, since our battles about his sauce américaine inspired it. At Le Bec-Fin, we made that sauce with lobster, bourbon, and a lot of cream and butter. The flavor was great, but it was so thick it could have passed for lobster bisque. I would suggest to Chef eliminating the fat and thickening the sauce with a little xanthan gum instead, and he'd react in horror. These are the things we fought about all the time. How to lighten. How to modernize. I'd win some, he'd win most, but all the back and forth helped me develop my point of view as a chef.

At Laurel, I can pay tribute to Chef's sauce américaine and the unparalleled flavor combination of lobster and bourbon in my own way. Our sauce is significantly lighter—out goes the pound of dairy, in goes a pound of seaweed—and the poached lobster tail and claw pick up some smoke and char on the grill while we brush them with apple-bourbon glaze. We pave the tail with crunchy grains, slivers of cured lobster roe, and the apple flowers that canopy our South Philly streets in pink and white petals as soon as the weather breaks in March.

This dish calls for four live lobsters, with roe purchased separately since it takes two weeks to cure. You need a tail and a claw for each portion, which means you'll have four claws left over. Some seafood suppliers sell cull (one-armed) lobsters, but having extra claws around isn't the worst problem. A suggestion from a native New Englander: make lobster rolls.

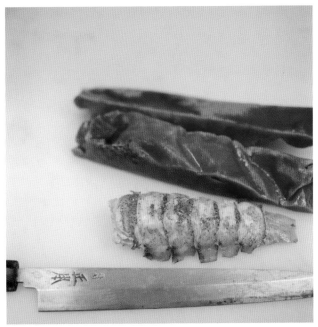

CURED LOBSTER ROE

8 ounces/227 g lobster roe
1 pound/454 g Kosher salt, divided

Set a circulator to 149°F. Purée the roe in a blender until smooth. Pass it through a chinois into a small vacuum bag, and seal on high. Cook sous vide for 2 hours. Shock the bag in ice water.

Fill a small pan with half the salt. Remove the roe from the bag, and lay it on top of the salt. Cover with the remaining salt, and cure for 1 hour. Remove the roe from the salt and rinse. Wrap it in cheesecloth, and hang it in the refrigerator for 2 weeks or until firm.

CRUNCHY GRAINS

3 cups/675 g grapeseed oil
6 ounces/180 g green farro
6 ounces/180 g wild rice
1 tablespoon/15 g Kosher salt, divided

Heat the oil in a large pot to 370°F. Line a shallow pan with paper towels, and set a chinois over a pot. When the oil reaches temperature, add the farro, and stir until the grains puff slightly, about 90 seconds. Carefully strain the farro through the chinois, reserving the hot oil. Immediately spread the farro on the paper towel–lined tray to cool. Season the farro with half the salt. Pour the oil back into the same pot, and reheat it to 370°F. Repeat the process with the wild rice, seasoning it with the remaining salt. Mix the grains together, and reserve in a cool, dry place.

BOURBON-APPLE GLAZE

8 ounces/250 g bourbon
4 ounces/115 g granulated sugar
2 cups/500 g freshly pressed apple juice

Combine the bourbon and the sugar in a small pot. Bring to a simmer, and reduce by half. Add the apple juice, and continue to reduce until the mixture becomes a thick, shiny syrup. Transfer it to a nonreactive airtight container and reserve cold.

LOBSTER AND SAUCE

4 live lobsters, 1.25 pounds/567 g each
1 pound/450 g fresh bladderwrack seaweed (if using dried bladderwrack, use half the amount)
8 ounces/225 g salt plus 1 pinch, divided
4 ounces/115 g grapeseed oil
½ bulb fennel, roughly chopped
2 shallots, sliced
4 garlic cloves, crushed
9 ounces/270 g bourbon, divided
2 quarts/2 L Lobster Stock (see page 155)
2 sprigs thyme
2 sprigs tarragon
2 tablespoons/20 g crushed black peppercorns
4 tablespoons/60 g unsalted butter

Hold a lobster securely by the body on a cutting board, and drive a knife through its head. Repeat for the remaining lobsters. Remove the tails and the claws, and place them in the refrigerator. Reserve the bodies for the sauce.

The following day, bring a large pot of water to a boil. Insert two metal skewers through each tail to keep them straight. Add the seaweed and 8 ounces/225 g salt to the water. Reduce the heat to a simmer, and add 4 claws. Poach for 5 minutes, then remove the claws and place them in the refrigerator. Add the tails, and poach for 4 minutes. Remove them from the water, and place them in the refrigerator. Once the claws and tails are cooled, use a pair of scissors to remove the shells. Pat the shelled meat dry with paper towels, and reserve it in the refrigerator. Discard the shells.

For the sauce, open up the bodies of the lobsters, and remove and discard any organs. Cut the shells into 2-inch/5-cm pieces. Warm the oil in a medium pot over high heat. Add the shells, and sauté them until they are deep red. Reduce the heat to medium, and add the fennel, shallots, and garlic. Cook until the vegetables are caramelized and soft, about 10

minutes. Increase the heat to high, and add 8 ounces of bourbon, scraping the bottom of the pot with a wooden spoon. Reduce the bourbon by half. Add the lobster stock, and bring the blend to a simmer, skimming off any impurities. Reduce the stock by two thirds, about 20 minutes. Strain the sauce through a chinois, being sure to press everything you can out of the shells. Add the thyme, tarragon, and black pepper, and steep in the sauce for 20 minutes. Strain the sauce through a chinois again into a clean pot. Add the butter and remaining bourbon, and emulsify with an immersion blender. Season with the remaining salt. Reserve warm.

TO PLATE

16 apple blossoms
24 anise hyssop leaves

Thinly slice 16 pieces of cured lobster roe. Warm the bourbon-apple glaze in a small saucepot over low heat, and start a charcoal grill. When the grill is hot, place the lobster tails and claws over direct heat. Brush the lobster with the glaze, and grill for 1 minute. Flip the lobster, glaze the opposite side, and grill for 1 minute. Remove the lobster from the grill, and cut off and discard the points of the claws. Press the presentation side of each tail into the crunchy grains, and place one tail on each of 4 plates. Garnish each tail with 4 slices of cured lobster roe, 4 apple blossoms, and 6 hyssop leaves. Add the claw portion to each plate. Aerate the lobster sauce with an immersion blender, and spoon 2 ounces/57 g of warm sauce around each portion.

FRESH RICOTTA GNOCCHI, BLACK TRUFFLE, TOASTED SOURDOUGH

My daughter, Grace, is a really adventurous eater. Her new thing is going to the library or bookstore to pick out cookbooks, and baking treats for the staff at Laurel. When she was a baby, everything had to be salted. She would eat jars of capers and olives, and by the time she was two, oysters and mussels and clams and other shellfish had joined the list. At some point, she turned into a starch monster; she craves it. We cook a lot of pasta at home. So when I was on *Top Chef* and there was a challenge to make a dish that reminded you of home, gnocchi were the first thing I thought of. I missed hanging out with my wife and cooking for my kids. I made these gnocchi, and the judges loved them.

A version of the *Top Chef* gnocchi is almost always a middle course of the tasting menu at Laurel. Once you master the basic pasta recipe, you can switch up the sauce however you like; the gnocchi are incredibly versatile. When I'm cooking at home, I don't have a secret stash of truffles I can raid on a random evening for the sauce, but D'Artagnan makes a high-quality and affordable truffle butter you can keep on hand in your freezer. That said, Grace won't be mad if you just toss the gnocchi in tomato sauce instead.

GNOCCHI

8 ounces/226 g ricotta
1 ounce/28 g all-purpose flour
1 egg yolk
1 tablespoon/15 g Kosher salt, plus more for cooking
    the gnocchi
Half bunch of chives, minced
Extra-virgin olive oil

Place the ricotta and the flour in the bowl of a stand mixer fitted with the paddle attachment, and combine on medium speed. With the mixer still running, slowly add the egg yolk and salt. Turn off the mixer, fold in the chives, and transfer the dough to a pastry bag. Rest the dough in the refrigerator for 2 hours.

Bring a large pot of water to a boil, and generously season with salt. Pipe out ½ inch of dough over the water, and snip it off with kitchen scissors. Continue this process for the rest of the dough, working quickly so the gnocchi don't overcook. Simmer the gnocchi for 2 minutes, constantly stirring the water. Skim the gnocchi from the water, drain well, toss in olive oil, and reserve on a sheet pan.

TO PLATE

4 tablespoons/60 g minced garlic
3 tablespoons/45 g extra-virgin olive oil
½ cup/118 ml water
3 ounces/85 g prepared white truffle butter, divided
.5 ounce/14.2 g cold unsalted butter
1 ounce/28 g lemon juice
Salt
Grated Grana Padano
Sourdough breadcrumbs
Grated black truffle

Combine the garlic and olive oil in a large sauté pan, and place over medium heat. Cook until the garlic softens, about 3 minutes; deglaze the pan with the water. Add the reserved gnocchi and half the truffle butter. Simmer for 1 minute to emulsify the sauce. Add the remaining truffle butter, and simmer for 1 minute more to emulsify the sauce. Add the cold butter, lemon juice, and salt to taste, and toss to combine. Transfer the gnocchi to a family-style serving platter, and garnish with grated Grana Padano, breadcrumbs, and grated black truffle.

BLACK TRUMPET MUSHROOM–STUFFED DOVER SOLE, CHICKEN JUS, WHEY ONIONS

Whole-roasted Dover sole is about as classic French as you can get. We prepared it all the time at Le Bec, presenting the fish and filleting it tableside. A lot of our early Laurel customers were Le Bec regulars, so I wanted to create a dish that was familiar but also surprising, something that made the statement "What we're doing here is different." This sole comes to the table looking like the original dish—we even present it on a floral grandma plate—and we cut it straight through the middle. The twist: instead of bones, black trumpet mushrooms.

To create the illusion, we skin and fillet a whole sole, leaving the fillets attached to the head. This lets us easily remove the skeleton, making the sole nearly boneless. We lay down a layer of sautéed and finely chopped mushrooms between the fillets and dust the whole fish with Activa, a protein bonder that often goes by the less appetizing nickname "meat glue." The name might conjure images of Frankenfoods, but Activa is way more practical than that. With this fish recipe—and you can replicate the technique with any whole fish of the same size, using any of a hundred different fillings—it lets us bond those fillets back together to create a cleaner, tighter, more flavorful bite.

STUFFED SOLE

6 ounces/170 g black trumpet mushrooms
1 tablespoon/15 g unsalted butter
1 sprig thyme
2 tablespoons/30 g Kosher salt, divided
1 teaspoon/5 g granulated sugar
Grated zest of 1 lemon
1 whole Dover sole, about 1 pound/454 g
2 tablespoons/20 g Activa

Pull the black trumpet mushrooms apart, being sure to check for pine needles. Submerge the mushrooms in room-temperature water, and swish them around to loosen any dirt. Remove the mushrooms from the water. Dump the water, and repeat the process until the water runs clear over the mushrooms. Gently squeeze out the excess water from the mushrooms, and pat them dry.

Meanwhile, brown the butter in a medium pot over medium heat. Add the thyme, cook for 1 minute, and then add the mushrooms. Add 1 tablespoon/15 g salt, and let the mushrooms cook until they release their liquid, about 5 minutes. Reduce the liquid completely, then season the mushrooms with the sugar and the lemon zest. Cool the mushrooms to room temperature in the pot. Reserve the four best-looking mushrooms. Chop the remaining mushrooms very finely, and reserve at room temperature.

Preheat the oven to 300°F. Score the skin at the tail end of the sole. Use a pair of fish tweezers and a paper towel to separate the skin from the flesh. In one quick motion, pull the skin toward the head of the fish, removing the skin entirely. Repeat on the opposite side of the fish. Scrape the inside of the skin clean with the back of a knife. Cut the skin into strips roughly measuring 2½ x ¾ inches/6 x 2 cm and bake them between 2 pieces of parchment until crispy, about 20 minutes. Reserve at room temperature.

Place the sole vertically on a cutting board with the head of the fish away from you. Use a fillet knife to remove the flesh of the fish from the skeleton while keeping the flesh attached to the head of the fish. Repeat on all 4 fillets of the fish. Use a pair of scissors to cut the skeleton away from the head. Reserve the bones for Chicken Jus (page 74). Season the fish all over with the remaining salt. Dust the fish all over with the Activa, and lightly pat the flesh with your hand to release any excess. Spoon a thin, even layer of the finely chopped mushrooms over the inside flesh of the fish. Place the fish in a large vacuum bag, and seal on low. Let the fish sit in the refrigerator for at least 6 hours for the flesh to fully adhere.

CHICKEN JUS

3 tablespoons/45 g grapeseed oil

2 chicken legs cut into 2-inch/5-cm pieces

2 teaspoons/10 g Kosher salt

Reserved sole bones

4 shallots, sliced

1 head garlic, split in half lengthwise

1 tablespoon/10 g cracked black pepper

3 sprigs thyme

1 cup/240 g brandy

1 cup/240 g pinot grigio

1 quart/1 L Roasted Chicken Stock (see page 156)

1 ounce/30 g truffle jus

1 tablespoon/15 g white soy sauce

2 tablespoons/30 g crème fraîche

Warm the grapeseed oil in a medium pot over high heat. Season the chicken with the salt, and sear on all sides until golden-brown, about 8 minutes. Remove the chicken from the pot and set aside. Add the fish bones to the pot, and sear until golden-brown, about 5 minutes. Remove the fish bones and set aside. Decrease the heat to medium, and add the shallot and the garlic, cut-side down; allow them to slowly brown, about 5 minutes. Add the black pepper and thyme. Place the chicken and fish bones back in the pot, increase the heat to high, and add the brandy. Stir the contents of the pot quickly with a wooden spoon to release any color on the bottom. Reduce the brandy until it is almost gone, and then add the pinot grigio. Reduce the wine by half, and stir in the chicken stock. Let the mixture simmer on low for about an hour. Strain the contents, return the liquid to the pot, and then reduce the sauce until it coats the back of a spoon. Season the sauce with the truffle jus and white soy sauce. Remove the pot from the heat, and whisk in the crème fraîche to emulsify. Reserve warm.

WHEY ONIONS

3 white onions

6 garlic cloves, thinly sliced

1 quart/1 L whey

Peel the onions, and cut them in half from top to bottom. Thinly slice the onions in the direction of the grain. Place the sliced onions in a medium pot with the garlic cloves and the whey. Bring the mixture to a simmer, and reduce slowly over medium heat until the onions are barely covered, about 15 minutes. Do not scorch. Use a potato masher to smash the onion and garlic. Continue to reduce the liquid until the onion-garlic mixture is mostly dry and can be formed into quenelles. Reserve warm.

TO PLATE

2 tablespoons/30 g unsalted butter, divided
1 tablespoon/15 g grapeseed oil
Black Shallots (see page 161)
Chive blossoms

Preheat the oven to 325°F. Remove the sole from the bag, and pat it dry with paper towels. In a large sauté pan, brown 1 tablespoon butter with the grapeseed oil. Lay the stuffed sole in the pan, and sauté it until golden-brown, about 1 minute. Flip the fish, and repeat on the other side. Transfer the fish to a rack set on a sheet pan, and bake it until the flesh feels firm to the touch and the fish is cooked through, about 5 minutes. Remove the sole from the oven, and let it rest 5 minutes.

While the sole is resting, warm the 4 whole mushrooms in a saucepan with the remaining butter over medium heat, about 3 minutes. Remove the head from the fish with a knife. Carve the body into 4 equal portions, and divide between 4 plates. Form 4 quenelles of whey onions by passing the mashed onions back and forth between 2 teaspoons. Add a quenelle to each plate, and top each quenelle with a 2-inch/5-cm slice of black shallot. Cover one side of each quenelle with chive blossoms. Top each piece of stuffed sole with a black trumpet mushroom and pieces of the reserved crispy fish skin. Spoon the chicken jus around each piece of sole.

HAY-CURED SQUAB EN VESSIE

Chef Perrier sent me to Guy Savoy in Paris to stage for a month in 2008. I would typically show up at seven thirty in the morning, work till the end of lunch at two, head back to my one-room flat for a nap, return to the restaurant at five thirty, work dinner service till one in the morning, go home, pass out, and do it all over again—and I loved it. It was there that I learned the technique of en vessie, or cooking ingredients in an inflated pig's bladder. En vessie is like the original sous vide. You're creating a steam chamber—sealing off a protein from the rest of the world so it can cook in its own juices. In this dish, we use one of my favorite animals, squab. We stuff the bodies with hay, then stuff those bodies into the bladder (ask your butcher), which gets inflated with a straw and tied closed tightly with twine. The inflated vessie floats like a beach ball in a shallow copper pot of chicken stock. For 20 minutes we continuously ladle the warm stock over the bladder, which continues to expand from the heat until it's straining against the twine and appears as though it's about to explode, like an overinflated balloon. Now for the fun part: we present the whole pan to the table, hold the vessie steady with tweezers, and pierce the top with a very sharp knife. There's no dramatic burst, but the aroma that wafts forward totally engulfs the table. Although the vessie definitely smells awful in its raw state (use your imagination), once stuffed and cooked according to this recipe, the scent is intoxicating: poultry and dry grass and barnyard and old wood. I get excited to make this dish just for that fragrance.

HAY-CURED SQUAB

1 squab, about 1 pound/454 g
3 tablespoons/45 g Kosher salt, divided
2 ounces/57 g hay
1 cup/225 g duck fat

Remove the legs from the squab, wrap them in plastic, and reserve chilled. Score the skin right above the anus, and pull the backbone down so that it breaks away from the cage. The intestinal tract and organs should pull away with the backbone. Clean any remaining organs from the cage of the bird, being sure to remove the lungs, heart, and liver. Clean the backbone and reserve. Remove the wings and neck from the cage, and reserve with the backbone. Season the inside and outside of the cage with half the salt, and pack it with the hay. Transfer the cage to a large vacuum bag and seal on high. Cure the cage in the refrigerator for 3 days.

After the cage has cured for 1 day, remove the legs from the fridge and season them with the remaining salt. Cure the legs for 6 hours in the refrigerator. After 6 hours, rinse the legs well, and pat dry with paper towels.

Melt the duck fat in a medium pot, and bring to 155°F. Add the legs, and cook for 6 hours at a consistent 155°F, checking for tenderness with a cake tester. Cool completely in the fat, and reserve cold until plating.

CELERY ROOT REDUCTION

1 large celery root
.4 ounces/10 g kombu
1 quart/1 L water
½ cup/113 g granulated sugar
1 teaspoon/5 g Kosher salt

Cut the celery root into ¾-inch/19-mm slices. Dehydrate at 120°F for 18 hours or until completely dry. Break up the slices into smaller pieces, and place them in a medium pot with the kombu and the water. Bring the mixture to a simmer, and cook for 15 minutes. Remove the pot from the heat, cover, and chill overnight, at least 12 hours. Strain off the solids, and return the liquid to the pot. Add the sugar, and reduce until thick and shiny. Season with the salt, and reserve warm.

GLAZED CELERY ROOT

1 pound/454 g celery root (peeling not necessary)
2 tablespoons/30 g extra-virgin olive oil
1 teaspoon/5 g Kosher salt
1 tablespoon/15 g unsalted butter
Celery Root Reduction (see above)
2 ounces/56.7 g baby mustard greens

Preheat the oven to 325°F. Scrub the celery root well, rub it with the olive oil, and season with the salt. Wrap the root in aluminum foil, and roast until tender, about 45 minutes. Unwrap the root and allow it to cool in the refrigerator. Cut into abstract pieces, roughly 1 x 1 inch/3 x 3 cm. Brown the butter in a medium sauté pan; add the celery root. Sauté over high heat until lightly browned on all sides. Add the celery root reduction, and continue to cook until the celery root pieces are glazed and shiny. Remove the pan from the heat, and add the mustard greens, gently stirring to lightly wilt. Reserve warm.

PICKLED ELDERBERRY JUS

1 tablespoon/15 g duck fat
Reserved squab bones
4 shallots, sliced
4 garlic cloves, crushed
1 pint/500 g zinfandel
1 piece kombu, 3 x 3 inches/8 x 8 cm
1 sprig thyme
1 quart/1 L Roasted Chicken Stock (see page 156)
1 cup Pickled Elderberries with their liquid (see page 158)

Warm the duck fat in a medium pot. Add the squab bones, and sauté until golden, about 5 minutes. Add the shallots and the garlic, and cook until caramelized, about 5 minutes. Add the wine, and reduce by half. Rinse the kombu and add it to the pot with the thyme and the chicken stock. Gently simmer undisturbed for 30 minutes, skimming off any impurities that rise. Strain through a chinois, and reduce until the sauce coats the back of a spoon. Season with enough elderberry pickling liquid to balance the sauce, about 1 to 1½ tablespoons/15 to 22 g. Add 40 elderberries. Reserve warm.

TO PLATE

1 pig bladder, rinsed under running water for 2 hours
Kosher salt
3 tablespoons/45 g truffle jus
2 tablespoons/30 g unsalted butter
3 quarts/3 L Roasted Chicken Stock (see page 156)
1 tablespoon/15 g grapeseed oil
1 tablespoon/15 g unsalted butter

Cut off the tip of the bladder, making a hole just large enough to allow you to insert the squab cage. Season the squab with salt. Insert it into the bladder with the truffle jus and the butter. Tie the bladder closed tightly with butcher's twine, and inflate it with a straw. Place the bladder in a deep pan with the chicken stock. Bring the stock to a simmer, continuously ladling the stock over the top of the bladder, which will expand like a balloon, for 20 minutes. Immediately present the bladder to the table in its cooking pan, and cut a slit in the top. Allow the bladder to deflate, and present the squab.

After presenting, take the pan back to the kitchen, carve the breasts from the cage, and season with the salt. Combine the grapeseed oil and the butter in a medium skillet over high heat. Set the confit legs and the breasts skin-side up in the pan, and cook for 10 seconds. Flip the breasts, and continue to cook, skin-side down, for 1½ minutes, basting continuously with the melted butter. Remove the squab from the pan, rest 4 minutes, and cut each breast and leg in half. Divide the squab pieces and glazed celery root between 2 plates. Garnish each portion with warm elderberry jus.

YUZU CURD, BLACK SESAME, TORCHED MALT CRISP

I suck at pastry. I mean, not *really*, but if you asked me to make a cake without a recipe, you'd wind up with something resembling a cake only in the most generous of terms. For chefs like me who came up in the classic French brigade system, desserts were someone else's responsibility. But for chefs like me who struck out on their own with a twenty-two-seat restaurant and a shoestring budget, well, tough shit. With no dedicated pastry chef, I started making desserts at Laurel based on what I knew. Eggs I know. The science of them, how they work. So a lot of the desserts here feature manipulations of egg: custards, curds, and creams, marshmallows and meringues. This one starts with a rich yuzu curd we lighten with whipped cream and set with gelatin into a wobbling, canary-yellow custard that looks like panna cotta. But unlike panna cotta, which tends to be dense and very dairy-forward, this thing is a lightning strike of citrus. I like to conclude my menus the same way I begin them, with acid, sending customers on their way feeling satisfied but invigorated, not like they need to immediately collapse on their beds.

MAKES 12 PORTIONS

YUZU CURD

6.75 sheets/20 g silver gelatin
2 cups/470 ml plus 2.7 ounces/75 g water
17.75 ounces/503 g heavy whipping cream
5.5 ounces/157 g egg yolk
11.5 ounces/325 g granulated sugar
4.4 ounces/125 g yuzu juice

Soak the gelatin in 2 cups/470 ml water for 5 minutes. While the gelatin is soaking, whip the cream in a stand mixer fitted with the whisk attachment to soft peaks; refrigerate. Squeeze the excess water out of the gelatin, and reserve at room temperature.

Place the yolks in a large mixing bowl, and whisk well. Combine the sugar and 2.7 ounces/75 g water in a small pot, and bring to a boil. Cook until the syrup reaches 246°F on a candy thermometer. Remove the pot from the heat. Slowly whisk the syrup into the egg mixture.

Combine the yuzu juice and the gelatin sheets in a small pot, and warm over low heat. When the gelatin has completely melted, whisk it into the egg mixture. Remove the whipped cream from the fridge, and, working in thirds, gently fold it into the yuzu-egg mixture. Cast the mix in an 8 x 8-inch/20 x 20-cm pan. Transfer it to the fridge, and let the curd cool until set, about 2 hours.

MALT CRISP

5.3 ounces/150 g granulated sugar
.5 ounce/15 g malt powder
½ teaspoon/2 g Kosher salt
4.4 ounces/125 g egg white

Purée all the ingredients in a blender until smooth. Spread the mixture on a sheet of acetate to .25-inch/.6-cm thick. Dehydrate at 120°F for 4 to 5 hours, until completely dry. Remove the crisp from the dehydrator, lightly toast it with a blowtorch, allow it to cool, and break it into large pieces with your hands. Reserve in a cool, dry place.

SESAME PASTE

2 ounces/56.7 g toasted black sesame seeds
4 ounces/113.4 g caster sugar
Pinch of Kosher salt

Grind the sesame seeds in a blender with the caster sugar to combine. Season with the salt, and reserve at room temperature.

OLIVE OIL–EGG GEL

2.1 ounces/60 g egg yolk
1.8 ounces/50 g glucose syrup
1.8 ounces/50 g Trimoline
8.8 ounces/250 g extra-virgin olive oil
Pinch of Kosher salt

Put the egg yolk in a blender, and blend on low until smooth. Bring the glucose and the Trimoline to a boil in a small pot. With the blender on low, slowly stream the hot glucose mixture into the egg yolks. Once the blend is completely emulsified, slowly add the olive oil, with the blender still running on low. When the mixture is completely emulsified and looks thick and shiny, season it with salt, cool to room temperature, and reserve at room temperature in a plastic squirt bottle.

TO PLATE

Maldon sea salt

Cut a 2.5-inch/6-cm round of yuzu curd, and set it in the bottom of a serving bowl. Top the curd with a thin layer of black sesame paste, then cover with the olive oil gel. Dust the gel with Maldon sea salt, and garnish with 4 shards of the malt crisp. Repeat for remaining portions.

COCKTAIL: THE KALI

You might think this magenta cocktail crowned with a glug of sparkling rosé took a wrong turn and wound up on our winter menu instead of our summer menu, but the Kali is most welcome when it's cold and gloomy outside. The color comes from hibiscus, the flower associated with the Hindu goddess that gives this drink its name, but the base is bourbon (preferably Wild Turkey 101), which brings some cold-weather gravitas without falling into the stereotype that all whiskey cocktails need to be heavy and alcoholic. With just half an ounce of liquor and about one ounce of wine, the Kali hits the right balance between sessionable and satisfying.

MAKES 1 COCKTAIL

HIBISCUS BOURBON

25.4 ounces/750 ml 101-proof bourbon
2.5 ounces/75 g dried hibiscus flowers

Combine the bourbon and the hibiscus in a bottle. Let it infuse in a cool, dry place for 2 days. Strain out the flowers, and rebottle.

TO SERVE

.5 ounce/15 ml Hibiscus Bourbon
.5 ounce/15 ml Lillet Blanc
.5 ounce/15 ml freshly squeezed lemon juice
.5 ounce/15 ml simple syrup
Sparkling rosé, to top

Pour the bourbon, Lillet, lemon juice, and simple syrup into a shaker, and dry shake for 10 seconds. Double strain the mixture into a double rocks glass over a large spherical ice cube. Top with sparkling rosé, and serve.

SPRING

Tonight We Are Serving

I.
Daylily Shoots, Dried Beef Heart

II.
Cardamom Leaf–Cured Bream,
Young and Old Peaches

III.
Wellfleet Oyster Cream, Pinelands Roots, Sochan

IV.
Steamed Pennsylvania Bamboo,
Egg, Chicken, Green Polenta

V.
Shaved Asparagus, Frog Leg Confit,
Wild Nettles, Jalapeño

VI.
Grilled Shrimp, Spring Ferments

VII.
Black Sea Bass, Peas, Rhubarb

VIII.
Braised Lamb Neck, Green Garlic, Ground Ivy Jus

IX.
Honeysuckle-Poached Rhubarb, Ice Cream,
Knotweed Jam, Lovage Granite

X.
Cocktail: A Bird Named Barb

DAYLILY SHOOTS, DRIED BEEF HEART

"Start tart" could be the motto of our fall and winter menus, where we want high acid and a little sugar because everything that follows goes deeper and deeper in flavor. The same is not true for spring. In this season, our kitchen pivots to fresh vegetal flavors, and there's less emphasis on taking guests' palates up and down through the menu. Instead, we focus more on riding a single wave across the subtle shades of green. Spring can show up unexpectedly early or late in the Delaware Valley, but by late April we're usually in a "Good-bye, root vegetable" groove. Ramps green our riverbanks, asparagus spears erupt from the dirt, and foragers like South Jersey's David Siller show up in the middle of dinner service, dragging twenty-pound trash bags of daylilies through the dining room. I love daylilies. David gets them young and tender for us, when they have a grassy, faintly sweet, light oniony flavor. One of the best ways to eat daylilies is barely wilted, which is how we open this spring menu, with a little dried beef heart grated over top for umami. Keep the leftover heart wrapped and stashed in the freezer; it's a fantastic finisher for vegetables, pasta, pizza, and salads.

MAKES 2 PORTIONS

1 beef heart, about 2 pounds/907 g
Kosher salt
2 daylily shoots
1 tablespoon/15 g unsalted butter

Cut the heart open, and remove any extraneous sinew and fat. Cut it into 2 x 5-inch/5 x 13-cm pieces. Place the pieces in a large vacuum bag with enough salt to cover all sides, and seal on high. Reserve cold for 3 weeks. Remove, rinse, and air dry the beef in a cool, dry place below 65°F for another 3 weeks or until it is very dark and very firm. Wrap it in plastic, and freeze for at least 2 hours before using.

Clean the daylily shoots of any dirt. In a medium sauté pan over medium heat, brown the butter. Add the shoots, and cook until they are just starting to wilt but remain crunchy, about 1 minute. Remove the shoots from the pan, and pat dry. Trim the tips. Transfer the shoots to a serving platter, and grate the dried beef heart over top. Serve while still warm.

CARDAMOM LEAF–CURED BREAM, YOUNG AND OLD PEACHES

Ben Wenk produces some of the best fruit in Pennsylvania. His farm, Three Springs, is located in Adams County, about two hours west of Philly, and he supplies Laurel with peaches from the tail end of spring through early fall. This dish originated in 2017, when Ben showed up with a basket of young green peaches and asked if we could do something with them. "Green" is a reference to the fruit's age, not the color (though they do have a pretty pale-jade hue), and they taste like a cross between a green almond and an unripe peach. On the farm, they're considered collateral damage; too many fruits on a branch spread the nutrients too thin, so Ben has to sacrifice some peaches early in the growing season to allow their branch-mates to fully ripen. We're able to take that product and turn it into something special—in this case, green peaches pickled in a sweet Champagne vinegar brine that highlights their flavor.

The peach pickles appear here as accents to sea bream cured with cardamom leaves, one of my favorite products from Green Meadow Farm in Lancaster County. The long, slender leaves are fibrous and intensely aromatic, with a perfume and flavor that are totally different from those of cardamom pods. Instead, you get these wild notes of bay and sweet pine and eucalyptus (which would make a lovely substitute) that go so well with fish—and with peaches. In addition to the pickled peaches, we plate the bream with white peach purée, salt-cured peaches, and white peach nage steeped with chamomile. So you have the whole life cycle of Ben's fruits represented in one dish: young peach, ripe peach, old peach.

MAKES 4 PORTIONS

SALTED PEACHES

4 pounds/2 kg Kosher salt, divided
1 pound/454 g ripe white peaches

Lay 1 pound/.5 kg of the salt down in a large nonreactive container. Place the whole peaches on top, making sure none of them are touching. Add another pound/.5 kg of salt; the peaches should be completely covered. Tightly cover and leave in a cool, dry place (below 65°F) for 2 weeks. Remove, rinse, and dry the peaches. Repeat the process to cure for another 2 weeks. Remove, rinse, and dry the peaches. Reserve cold.

PICKLED GREEN PEACHES

1 quart/1 L Champagne vinegar
2½ cups/500 g granulated sugar
1½ quarts/1.4 L water
1 pound/454 g baby green peaches, about half-dollar size

Combine the vinegar and sugar with the water in a medium pot, and cook over medium heat until the sugar has dissolved. Cool completely. Pour the pickling liquid over the peaches in a sterilized, nonreactive, airtight container, and cover. Leave in a cool, dry place for 2 weeks.

WHITE PEACH AND CHAMOMILE NAGE

4 ripe white peaches
1 quart/1 L water
2 tablespoons/5 g dried chamomile flowers
1 teaspoon/5 g honey
Grated zest and juice of 1 lime
¼ teaspoon/1.3 g Kosher salt

Slice the peaches very thin, and dehydrate for 2 hours at 125°F or until they are completely dry but not colored. Heat the water to 190°F. Place the dehydrated peaches, chamomile, and honey in a nonreactive airtight container. Pour the hot water over the contents, and cover. Steep overnight in the fridge. Strain the following day, discarding the solids, and season the liquid with the lime zest, lime juice, and salt. Reserve cold.

PEACH PURÉE

1 pound/454 g ripe white peaches

Set a circulator to 190°F. Peel and pit the peaches, transfer to a large vacuum bag, and seal on high. Cook sous vide for 30 minutes or until the flesh breaks down. Cool, and purée until smooth. Transfer the purée to a plastic squeeze bottle, and reserve cold.

TO PLATE

4 ounces/120 g Kosher salt
5 cardamom leaves
1 skinned fillet of sea bream, about 8 ounces/227 g
28 bachelor's button flowers
24 chamomile greens

Pulse the salt and cardamom leaves in a food processor until well combined. Season the bream on both sides with the salt mixture, and cure for 20 minutes in the fridge. Rinse the bream, pat dry, and cut in ¼-inch/6-mm dice. Divide the diced bream into 4 equal portions. Place 1 tablespoon/5 g of peach purée in the bottom of a bowl, and top with 1 portion of bream. Finely dice 1 salted peach. Garnish the bream with 7 small pieces of the salted peach. Thinly slice 4 pickled green peaches. Top each piece of salted peach with a slice of pickled peach. Garnish with 7 bachelor's buttons and 6 chamomile greens. Spoon 1 ounce/30 g of the white peach nage around the fish. Repeat for remaining portions, and serve immediately.

WELLFLEET OYSTER CREAM, PINELANDS ROOTS, SOCHAN

The Wellfleet is my favorite oyster, and not just because we're both from Massachusetts. Raised in swift-moving saltwater, Wellfleets taste like the ocean, as crisp and briny as the crack of a wave. In this course we gently warm the oysters with olive oil and sochan, a native North American plant whose leaves remind me of celery, and hide them under a cool and fluffy oyster cream. Diane Gabler of Pinelands Produce grows the sochan for us. She's a former nurse who started farming her land in Brown Mills, New Jersey, a few years ago. Diane grows whatever rare and strange herb we ask her to (wood sorrel, shungiku, sunflower sprouts), as well as pristine specimens of familiar crops like beets, turnips, and radishes, all of which appear as raw garnishes in this dish. If you can't get your hands on sochan, lovage works well as a substitute.

OYSTERS

8 Wellfleet oysters
2 sprigs sochan
2 tablespoons/30 g extra-virgin olive oil

Set a circulator to 128°F. Shuck the oysters, being careful not to puncture the bellies. Rinse them, and place them in a small vacuum bag. Lightly crush the sochan in your hand and add it to the bag with the olive oil. Seal on high, and place the bag in the water bath. Cook for 20 minutes. Shock the bag in ice water to cool the contents, and reserve the oysters in the bag until plating.

OYSTER CREAM

8.4 ounces/250 g whole milk
4 ounces/125 g heavy whipping cream
1½ teaspoons/4.5 g agar-agar
6 Wellfleet oysters, shucked and rinsed
1 teaspoon/5 g salt

Pour the milk and cream into a small pot, and whisk in the agar. Bring the mixture to a simmer, whisking constantly, and simmer for 2 minutes. Remove the pot from the heat, and let the temperature drop to 150°F. Purée the oysters in a blender, slowly streaming in the warm milk and cream. Pass the mixture through a chinois, and let it set in a cool place. Purée the mixture, and season it with the salt. Load it into a plastic squeeze bottle, and chill.

TO PLATE

1 daikon radish
Maldon sea salt
1 small white turnip, very thinly shaved
1 small Easter egg radish, very thinly shaved
1 small gold beet, very thinly shaved
32 baby red shiso leaves
Sochan Powder (see page 162)
Olio Verde

Trim the daikon to measure 8 inches/20 cm in length, and peel it. Using a vegetable sheeter, roll out two 4-foot/1-m strips. Cut each strip in half to create four 2-foot/.6-m strips, and trim the sides so each measures ¾ inch/2 cm wide. Season the daikon with Maldon, and set it aside for 5 minutes. Lay out the daikon strips flat, and arrange alternating slices of turnip, Easter egg radish, and beet along the surface of each strip. Place 1 tablespoon/20 g of oyster cream in the middle of a plate, and top it with 1 oyster. Pick up a strip of daikon; the slices of turnip, radish, and beet will stick to it. Arrange it like a nest over the oyster. Top the nest with another oyster and 2 dots of oyster cream. Garnish with 8 shiso leaves, powdered sochan, 5 drops of Olio Verde, and a sprinkle of Maldon. Repeat for remaining portions, and serve immediately.

STEAMED PENNSYLVANIA BAMBOO, EGG, CHICKEN, GREEN POLENTA

Some dishes start out clearly formed in my head. Other times, I just get lucky. This course is a case of the latter. We had been using bamboo, fried green polenta sticks, and this very robust Champagne-spiked chicken broth in separate dishes, and one day we decided to try plating them together. It made so much sense. As we started building the new dish out of the various elements, it took on the appearance of a nest, with the polenta and bamboo encircling a sous vide egg yolk. When you break the yolk and it bleeds into the chicken broth, which we pour tableside, the combo becomes a silky sauce that's a perfect foil for the subtle funkiness of the bamboo. Considering the broth, which we use to make the polenta as well as to finish the dish, and the egg, you could think that this plate is an ode to chicken, but it's really all about the bamboo, an ingredient I love. It's invasive and grows everywhere here, but I never knew there was Pennsylvania bamboo you could eat until our forager David Siller brought us some from Mullica Hill, in New Jersey. With bamboo, the younger the better. It should have a fat base and be no taller than a foot above ground; anything older and it gets bitter and astringent.

MAKES 4 PORTIONS

CHAMPAGNE CHICKEN BROTH

1 tablespoon/15 g grapeseed oil
1 pound/450 g chicken wings
2 shallots, sliced
½ head garlic
1 cup/250 g Champagne
2 quarts/2 L Roasted Chicken Stock (see page 156)
½ tablespoon/8 g koji extract
½ tablespoon/8 g kelp extract

Warm the oil in a large pot over medium heat. Add the wings, and brown them all over. Add the shallots and garlic, and cook until the shallots become translucent, about 2 minutes. Add the Champagne, and reduce to dry, about 4 minutes. Add the chicken stock, and bring to a boil. Lower the heat to a simmer, and cook for 1 hour, skimming off any impurities. Strain the broth, discard the solids, and return the broth to medium heat. Reduce by one-third, about 15 minutes, after which the broth will have a golden color and an intense flavor. Remove the broth from the heat, and stir in the koji and kelp extracts. Reserve warm.

GREEN POLENTA CRISPS

3 cups/750 g Champagne Chicken Broth
    (see page 104)
1 cup/200 g green polenta
2.5 teaspoons/13 g Kosher salt, divided
16 ounces/450 g canola oil

Pour the warm broth into a medium pot, and whisk in the polenta. Place the pot over medium heat, and bring the liquid to a simmer, whisking constantly. Continuing to whisk, allow the mixture to simmer until the polenta is cooked and has absorbed all the liquid, about 20 minutes. Stir in 2 teaspoons/10 g of the salt and, working quickly, transfer the polenta to a small piping bag. Pipe out thin 6-inch/15-cm strips of the polenta onto acetate paper. Dehydrate the strips at 120°F for 6 hours or until completely dried. Heat the oil in a deep pot to 350°F. Add the polenta sticks, and fry until crisp, about 10 seconds. Season with the remaining salt, and reserve in a cool, dry place.

EGGS

4 eggs, at room temperature

Set a circulator to 145°F. Cook the eggs sous vide for 1 hour and 15 minutes. Peel the eggs, and reserve at room temperature.

TO PLATE

8 stalks young bamboo
Maldon sea salt
Olio Verde

Wash the bamboo well. Cut away and discard the tough outer layer of each stalk, reserving just the shoot. Cut each shoot in half lengthwise, and steam until tender, about 3 minutes. While the bamboo is steaming, set out 4 bowls. Peel away the whites from the eggs, and gently set a warm yolk in the center of each bowl. Season the bamboo with the salt, and cut the stalks into 1½-inch/4-cm-long batons. Form a nest around each yolk with 8 pieces of bamboo and 6 polenta sticks. Season each yolk with 5 drops of Olio Verde and a sprinkle of salt. Gently pour ½ cup/125 g broth over each yolk tableside.

SHAVED ASPARAGUS, FROG LEG CONFIT, WILD NETTLES, JALAPEÑO

When we went tasting-only in 2015, we decided not to give out menus until the end of the meal. We want our customers to be surprised and delighted by the progression of courses. We also want them to try things they might normally avoid, like frog legs. In my experience, frog legs are not something most people get psyched to eat, and I've been attempting for years to come up with a treatment that makes them undeniably delicious. We hit on this preparation last spring: we make a confit instead of using the typical method of pan-roasting or deep-frying them, and we pair them with garlicky nettles, forms of asparagus, herb butter, and a jalapeño purée that's more sweet than hot. Cured with brown sugar and cooked sous vide with duck fat, frog legs ditch the "tastes like chicken" comparison. Instead they taste like slowly cooked bass—delicious. Frogs live in the water after all.

If you live in the South, sourcing frog legs shouldn't be a problem. The ones we use at Laurel come from Florida. In other parts of the country, check the nearest Asian supermarket. Take care when picking the delicate meat off the bones after cooking them; you want bite-sized pieces that won't get lost among the other elements. This is definitely a frog leg–centric dish. We just don't always want our guests to know that.

MAKES 4 PORTIONS

WHITE ASPARAGUS GLAZE

1 pound/454 g white asparagus, chopped into
  ½-inch/1-cm pieces
1 tablespoon/15 g Kosher salt
Juice of 1 lime
1½ teaspoons/4 g xanthan gum

Purée the chopped asparagus and the salt together in a food processor. Transfer the purée to a large vacuum bag, and seal on high. Leave the bag out at room temperature for 3 days or until the bag puffs. Strain the liquid from the bag, and discard the solids. Whisk the lime juice into the liquid, and add the xanthan. Purée with an immersion blender, pass through a chinois, and reserve at room temperature.

FROG LEGS

4 ounces/114 g Kosher salt
1 ounce/28 g packed dark brown sugar
1 pound/454 g frog legs, skinned
2 sprigs thyme
1 tablespoon/14 g duck fat

Whisk the salt and sugar together in a bowl. Clean and separate the frog legs from the backs. Season the legs well with the salt, and cure for 1 hour in the fridge. Rinse the legs well after curing, and set a circulator to 135°F. Wrap the thyme in a coffee filter or cheesecloth, and tie it closed. Place the frog legs, duck fat, and thyme in a large vacuum bag, and seal on high. Cook sous vide for 1 hour or until the legs are tender. Cool the bag in an ice bath. When the frog legs are cool enough to handle, carefully pick the meat from the legs, leaving the pieces as large as possible. Reserve warm.

GARLIC NETTLES

1 cup garlic cloves
1 tablespoon/14 g crème fraîche
2½ teaspoons/12 g Kosher salt, divided
2 pounds/907.2 g stinging nettles

Cover the garlic cloves with water in a medium pot. Bring the liquid to a simmer, then immediately strain out the water. Repeat this process 8 times, changing the water each time. After the final simmer, strain very well, and pat the garlic dry. Purée the garlic in a blender until smooth, pass it through a chinois, and cool. Stir in the crème fraîche and 1 teaspoon/5 g of the salt. Transfer the blend to a plastic squeeze bottle, and reserve at room temperature.

Carefully pick the leaves from the nettle stems, wearing gloves (several pairs, if you're using thin latex gloves) to protect your hands. Discard the stems. Rinse the leaves in ice water 3 times to remove any debris. Dry the leaves well. Steam the leaves in 2 batches for 4 minutes per batch. Lay the leaves flat on a sheet pan lined with parchment, and cool them in the refrigerator. Chop the nettles well, and stir in the remaining salt and 1 tablespoon/15 g of the garlic purée. Reserve at room temperature.

JALAPEÑO PURÉE

8 ounces/250 g jalapeño peppers, seeds and ribs removed
1.9 ounces/50 g flat-leaf parsley leaves
1.9 ounces/50 g basil leaves
16 ounces/500 g grapeseed oil
1.9 ounces/50 g Trimoline
1.9 ounces/50 g glucose syrup
2 ounces/60 g egg yolk

Rinse the seeded jalapeños well in cold water, and purée them in a blender with the parsley, basil, and grapeseed oil until the mixture is smooth and very warm. Pass the blend through a chinois, and reserve the oil at room temperature. Bring the Trimoline and glucose to boil in a small pot. Pour the hot mixture into a food processor, and, with the processor running, add the egg yolk to emulsify. Slowly stream in the jalapeño oil. Transfer the mixture to a medium vacuum bag, seal on high, then immediately open it to disperse any air bubbles. Repeat this process 2 more times. Transfer the purée to a plastic squeeze bottle, and reserve at room temperature.

HERB BUTTER

2 teaspoons/10 g Kosher salt
3 ounces/85 g chervil leaves
3 ounces/85 g flat-leaf parsley leaves
3 ounces/85 g tarragon leaves
3 ounces/85 g basil leaves
1 teaspoon/3 g xanthan gum
1 cup/237 ml water
2 pounds/900 g unsalted butter, cubed

Bring a large pot of water to a boil, and add the salt. Blanch the herbs in the boiling water for 4 minutes, then shock them in ice water. Squeeze out the excess water, and purée the herbs in a blender until smooth. Reserve cold.

Purée the xanthan and the water in a blender for 1 minute. Transfer the mixture to a medium pot, and bring it to a simmer. Whisk the butter into the xanthan mixture one cube at a time. Measure 8 tablespoons/120 g of the butter-xanthan mixture into a separate pot, and whisk in 4 tablespoons/60 g of the herb purée. Reserve warm.

TO PLATE

16 spears asparagus
Kosher salt
1 tablespoon/15 g unsalted butter
Black locust flowers

Cut 12 spears of asparagus into 4.5-inch/11-cm-long pieces. Shave the asparagus pieces lengthwise on a mandoline to a thickness of $\frac{1}{16}$ inch/2 mm. Season the shaved asparagus with salt, and allow it to rest until it becomes pliable, about 20 minutes. Meanwhile, sauté the remaining spears of asparagus in the butter until al dente, about 2 minutes; reserve warm. Rinse and dry the shaved asparagus, and brush it with the white asparagus glaze. Set out 4 deep bowls, and place 1 tablespoon/15 g of garlic nettles in each. Divide the frog leg confit among the bowls, and top each portion of meat with 1 roasted spear of asparagus and 6 dots of jalapeno purée. Top each bowl with the shaved asparagus. Pour 3 tablespoons/45 g herb butter around each portion, and garnish with black locust flowers.

GRILLED SHRIMP, SPRING FERMENTS

We order fruits and vegetables and herbs like any other restaurant, but our farmers and foragers also just show up with stuff. This is how we were introduced to toothwort, a root from the horseradish family. Forager Evan Strusinski showed up with a bunch of the long, beige, bristly root three years ago. When we get something new like this, the first thing we do is taste it raw. Raw toothwort tasted like nothing beyond a super-mellow hint of horseradish. The second thing we do is brine or ferment it for a couple of days. The toothwort still didn't taste like much. So we brined a whole batch of toothwort, stuck it on a shelf in the basement with the rest of our pickles and ferments, and forgot about it for two years. One day when we were doing inventory, we came across it, opened the jar, and fell hard. Spending two years in brine woke up the horseradish flavor and turned the toothwort's texture into that of a starchy root vegetable.

We're always developing new dishes, but perfecting one for the menu can take a long time, which is why keeping a well-rounded larder is essential. When we need to come up with something on the fly, we start downstairs with our pickles and ferments. It's nice having a robust inventory we can pull from, because we already know what those items taste like and how each one will work with other elements. That's what happened here. We had a grilled-shrimp dish with an intense shrimp-head butter—all oceanic sweetness and fat—that needed acid and salt. Walk downstairs. Grab the toothwort along with other spring ferments—some from the current season, like radish tops, which take only a couple of days to get funky, and others from previous years, like Hercules' club. Problem solved.

If you can't find foraged plants like toothwort or Hercules' club or the daylilies we turn into quick kimchi, just go with all radish tops, or ferment a mix of radish tops, mustard greens, and beet greens. You can also use high-quality, young, store-bought kimchi.

MAKES 6 PORTIONS

BRINED TOOTHWORT

1 pound/454 g toothwort
1.7 ounces/47 g Kosher salt
1 quart/1 L water

Clean the toothwort of any dirt, and place it in a sterilized glass 1-quart/1-L jar. Add the salt to the water in a medium pot, and bring it to a simmer, stirring to dissolve the salt. Pour the brine over the toothwort, and seal the jar. Brine in a cool, dark place for 1 year.

FERMENTED HERCULES' CLUB

1 pound/454 g Hercules' club
.5 ounce/14 g Kosher salt

Toss the Hercules' club with the salt. Transfer to a medium vacuum bag, seal on high, and reserve in a cool, dry place for 4 days. Reserve cold.

FERMENTED RADISH TOPS

1 pound/454 g radish tops
.4 ounce/11 g Kosher salt

Toss the radish tops with the salt. Transfer to a medium vacuum bag, seal on high, and allow to ferment in a cool, dry place for 4 days. Reserve cold.

DAYLILY KIMCHI

1 pound/454 g daylily shoots
1 shallot, thinly sliced
2 inches/5 cm fresh ginger, grated
Kosher salt

Clean the daylily shoots of any dirt, thinly slice, and combine them with the shallot and the ginger. Weigh the mix, and calculate 2.5 percent of the weight in salt. Toss the salt with the mix, and transfer it to a large vacuum bag. Seal on high, and leave at room temperature for 3 to 4 days, after which the lilies will have softened and paled in color. Remove the mix from bag, and finely chop. Reserve ¼ cup/60 g at room temperature for plating. Transfer the excess to a nonreactive airtight container, and reserve cold for future use.

SHRIMP BUTTER

6 tablespoons/90 g unsalted butter, divided
Heads from 6 U-12 shrimp
1 shallot, thinly sliced
1 garlic clove, thinly sliced
1 cup/250 g Chablis
1 sprig tarragon
1 sprig lemon thyme
1 quart/1 L water
1 teaspoon/5 g Kosher salt

Place 2 tablespoons/30 g butter and the shrimp heads in a medium pot over medium heat. Use a potato masher to crush the heads as they caramelize with the butter. Cook until the shrimp heads turn bright red, about 5 minutes. Add the shallot and the garlic, and cook for 8 minutes. Add the wine and deglaze the pan, scraping up any brown bits stuck to the bottom. Reduce until the wine has evaporated, about 3 minutes. Add the herbs and the water; reduce by half, about 20 minutes. Strain the liquid, discarding the solids, and reduce again until strongly flavored, about 10 minutes. Season with the salt, and whisk in the remaining butter. Strain again, and reserve warm.

TO PLATE

6 head-on U-12 shrimp, peeled and deveined
1 tablespoon/15 g grapeseed oil
1 tablespoon/15 g unsalted butter, at room
    temperature
1 teaspoon/5 g Kosher salt

Slide a metal skewer through the length of each shrimp. Light a grill and get the coals glowing hot. Cut 3 fermented Hercules' clubs in half lengthwise, and combine them in a small skillet with 6 1-inch/3-cm pieces of brined toothwort and the grapeseed oil. Sauté over medium heat for 4 minutes. Cut 3 fermented radish tops in half lengthwise, and add them to the pan to warm through for 1 minute. Remove the pan from the heat, and transfer the contents to a paper towel to absorb the excess oil.

Lightly brush the shrimp with the butter, and season them with salt on both sides. Grill until just medium-rare, about 1 minute on each side, and remove the skewer. Remove the heads, and reserve for plating. Place each shrimp in a shallow bowl next to its head. Carefully spoon 2 teaspoons/10 g of the daylily kimchi on top of each shrimp. Garnish each with the warm spring ferments. Spoon warm shrimp butter around each portion and serve.

BLACK SEA BASS, PEAS, RHUBARB

Black sea bass is such a delicate fish. Basically, once it's warm, it's ready to go. We achieve that by curing the fish well, warming it just to the right temperature, putting it on a hot plate, and pouring a hot sauce over it. If those steps are done properly in a timely manner, the fish just falls apart. Since this recipe calls for fillets and bones, buying a whole bass is the most economical option.

Peas start popping in Pennsylvania in late May, and this course features several varieties. Snap peas get roasted until thoroughly charred, then buzzed into a powder that gives the bass a marbled look. English peas and pea leaves meet in a purée. Shelled peas join pistachios and tarragon in a quick sauté with butter, favas, and iridescent beads of finger lime. This supporting cast of peas grounds the bass, while rhubarb "raisins" punch up the acidity and introduce an unexpected texture. The raisin trick is inspired by my son Wesley's love of gummy candies (gummy sharks, in particular). Rhubarb turns to mush when you cook it, but if you do it sous vide very slowly, you can preserve its integrity. After cooking, you chop and dehydrate it, then rehydrate it in a rhubarb and green strawberry syrup. You wind up with these chewy little raisins that are sweet, sour, and delicious on everything from sundaes to cereal to fancy Ants on a Log.

MAKES 4 PORTIONS

RHUBARB RAISINS

7 ounces/200 g water
7 ounces/200 g plus 2 tablespoons/20g granulated
    sugar, divided
3 pounds/1.4 kg rhubarb, divided
8 ounces green strawberries
1 teaspoon/2 g citric acid

Set a circulator to 145°F. Heat the water and 7 ounces/200 g of the sugar over medium heat until the sugar has dissolved. Cool completely. Peel the red skin off the rhubarb, and place 2 pounds/1 kg of it in a large vacuum bag with the sugar water; seal on high. Cook the rhubarb for 45 minutes or until tender. Cool. Slice it into pieces that are ½ inch/1 cm thick, and dehydrate for 12 hours at 120°F.

After the rhubarb has been dehydrated, juice the green strawberries and the remaining 1 pound/400 g of fresh rhubarb. Whisk in the citric acid and the remaining sugar until dissolved. Soak the dehydrated rhubarb in the juice until rehydrated, about 30 minutes. Strain the rhubarb raisins from the liquid, and reserve at room temperature.

PEA ASH

8 ounces/227 g snap peas

Roast the snap peas dry in a 400°F oven for 6 hours, after which they should be completely dry and black. Cool. Grind the peas into a powder, and reserve in a mesh-top shaker.

SAUCE

1 whole black bass, about 2.5 pounds/1 kg
2 shallots, sliced
½ bulb fennel, sliced
1 leek, sliced
3 sprigs thyme
2 bay leaves
1 quart/1 L water
½ cup/120 g heavy whipping cream
1 tablespoon/17 g tamari

Skin and fillet the bass, reserving the fillets cold for plating. Rinse the skeleton under cold running water for 1 hour, then add it to a medium pot with the shallots, fennel, leek, thyme, bay leaves, and water. Simmer for 30 minutes, skimming off any impurities. Strain out the solids, and return the liquid to the pot. Add the cream and bring to a boil. Stir in the tamari and reserve warm.

PEA PURÉE

1 pound/455 g English peas
4 ounces/113 g pea leaves
1 tablespoon/15 g Kosher salt, plus more for blanching

Blanch the peas in boiling salted water until cooked through, about 3 minutes. Remove the peas with a strainer, reserving the blanching water, and shock the peas in ice water. Blanch the pea leaves in the same boiling water until completely soft, about 4 minutes. Remove them with a strainer, and shock them in ice water. Purée the peas and the leaves. Season with the salt, and transfer the purée to a squeeze bottle. Reserve at room temperature.

TO PLATE

Reserved bass fillets
2 teaspoons/10 g Kosher salt
4 ounces/120 g shelled peas
4 ounces/120 g shelled and peeled fava beans
½ cup/100 g raw shelled pistachios
2 tablespoons/30 g unsalted butter
Pulp of 2 finger limes
2 tablespoons/20 g trout roe
2 tablespoons/6 g brunoised tarragon
12 pea greens
8 pea flowers

Preheat the oven to 350°F. Season the bass fillets with the salt, and cure for 15 minutes in the refrigerator. Rinse, pat dry, and coat the bass on both sides with the pea ash. Slice the bass ½ inch/1 cm thick, and divide the slices into 4 portions. On a piece of waxed paper, arrange a portion of slices together into a circular mosaic roughly 3 inches/8 cm in diameter. Repeat for the remaining portions, for a total of 4 disks of bass.

Place the peas, favas, and pistachios in a small pot with the butter and a splash of water, and bring to a simmer, cooking until the peas and favas are tender, about 2 minutes. Use a slotted spoon to transfer the contents of the pot to a paper towel to absorb excess fat. In a small serving bowl, stir together the pea mixture with the finger lime, trout roe, and tarragon.

Warm the disks of bass in the oven for 2 minutes. Remove and set one of them in the center of a hot plate. Garnish with 8 dots pea purée, 5 rhubarb raisins, 3 pea greens, and 2 pea flowers. Repeat for the remaining disks of bass. Foam the warm sauce with an immersion blender, skim off 8 large spoonfuls of foam, and gently fold the foam into the bowl of peas, favas, and roe. Spoon the mix over each portion of bass and serve immediately.

BRAISED LAMB NECK, GREEN GARLIC, GROUND IVY JUS

Ground ivy goes by many names—catfoot, creeping charlie, gill-over-the-ground, runaway robin—but this invasive cousin of mint has a scent that is singular: lamb. Really, it smells like beautiful, slowly cooked lamb. The first time we smelled it, we were so knocked out by the similarity that we built this whole dish around the plant. The ivy flavors both the cure for the lamb and the lamb sauce that accompanies the meat—"lamb" on lamb on lamb. If that doesn't communicate spring well enough, this course continues to rep the season with additions of caramelized green garlic, fermented garlic scapes, ramp tops, and elderflowers.

We work with lamb neck for this recipe, which isn't the actual neck of the animal but the trap muscle. It comes in neat tubes that are easy to portion and ideal to braise. At Laurel we do a reverse braise, curing the meat for a specific amount of time, slowly cooking it sous vide or in the CVap, then searing and glazing it in a pan to finish. (Unless I'm making lamb shanks or short ribs for my kids at home, when I use the traditional method, this is how I braise.) This dish doesn't work unless you use high-quality lamb. With delicate lamb, you can intensify the flavor without it becoming off-putting. Try this recipe with gamy lamb, and it won't taste very appealing. We get ours from Idaho through D'Artagnan, which you can order online, or ask around at your local farmers' market. American lamb tends to be much less gamy than the meat shipped here from Australia and New Zealand.

MAKES 4 PORTIONS

LAMB FLOSS

1 lamb shank, about 8 ounces/227 g
2 tablespoons/30g Kosher salt
1 tablespoon/15 g grapeseed oil
1 tablespoon/15 g extra-virgin olive oil

Set a circulator to 154°F. Season the lamb with the salt and brown it with the grapeseed oil in a medium pot over high heat. Cool the lamb to room temperature. Transfer it to a large vacuum bag with the olive oil and seal on high. Cook for 48 hours. Cool and rinse the lamb. Pick the meat off the bone, and dehydrate it at 120°F for 8 hours. Pulse the meat in a food processor until it is light and fluffy. Reserve at room temperature in a nonreactive airtight container.

LAMB NECKS

4 ounces/112 g Kosher salt
2 ounces/57 g packed light brown sugar
2 bay leaves
3 sprigs ground ivy
1 sprig tarragon
2 8-ounce/227-g lamb necks
1 tablespoon/15 g grapeseed oil

Make the cure by combining the salt, sugar, bay leaves, ground ivy, and tarragon in a food processor and pulsing until well combined. Season the lamb with the cure, and let it rest for 12 hours.

Set a circulator to 147°F. Rinse the lamb, and transfer it to a large vacuum bag with the grapeseed oil. Seal on high, and cook the lamb sous vide for 48 hours. Remove the bagged lamb from the water bath, and allow it to cool to room temperature for 1 hour. Transfer the bag to ice water for 1 hour. Reserve cold.

GROUND IVY JUS

1½ tablespoons/23 g grapeseed oil
½ pound/227 g lamb leg cubes
1 teaspoon/5 g Kosher salt
½ white onion, sliced
2 shallots, sliced
½ head garlic
1 tablespoon/14 g granulated sugar
1 tablespoon/14 g red wine vinegar
1 cup/250 g merlot
1 quart/1 L Lamb Stock (see page 155)
1 tablespoon/15 g unsalted butter
12 ounces/340 g ground ivy

Heat the oil in a medium pot over high heat until almost smoking. Season the lamb with the salt, and sauté it until golden-brown. Add the onion, shallots, and garlic, and reduce the heat to low. Caramelize the vegetables until soft. Raise the heat, add the sugar, and cook until deep brown. Add the vinegar, and reduce until dry. Add the merlot a little at a time, scraping with a wooden spoon to release any browned bits at the bottom of the pan. Reduce the wine to dry, and add the lamb stock. Simmer for 30 minutes. Strain through a chinois, discard the solids, and return the liquid to a clean pot. Reduce until the liquid coats the back of a spoon. Whisk the butter into the sauce. Place the ground ivy in a deep pot. Pour the sauce over the ivy, and allow it to steep for 20 minutes. Pass through a chinois and reserve warm.

CARAMELIZED GREEN GARLIC

1 ounce/29 g grapeseed oil
1 pound/454 g green garlic, chopped
½ tablespoon/8 g unsalted butter

Warm the oil over medium heat and add the garlic. Slowly cook the garlic until it is caramelized, adding splashes of water as needed to prevent the garlic from getting too deeply colored, about 45 minutes. Stir in the butter and reserve warm.

TO PLATE

1 tablespoon/15 g unsalted butter
4 teaspoons/20 g grapeseed oil, divided
4 salsify flowers
4 ramp tops, split lengthwise
Fermented Garlic Scapes (see page 162)
48 elderflowers

Bring 8 ounces/240 g of the ivy jus up to a simmer. Remove the lamb necks from the bag and cut each piece in half, for a total of 4 portions. Caramelize the lamb necks over high heat in a small sauté pan with the butter and 1 tablespoon/15 g of the grapeseed oil, 2 minutes total, flipping halfway through. Add the lamb necks to the ivy jus, and allow the meat to warm through. Very quickly wilt the salsify flowers and ramp tops in a small sauté pan with the remaining oil, dab them on a paper towel to absorb excess oil, and split the salsify flowers lengthwise. Place 2 teaspoons/15 g of the caramelized garlic on a plate, and top with a portion of lamb neck. Spoon 1 tablespoon/10 g fermented scapes in a stripe along the top of the lamb, and drape with the wilted ramp tops and salsify flowers. Set 1 tablespoon/3 g lamb floss next to the lamb, and spoon 1 tablespoon/15 g ivy jus around the plate. Garnish with about 1 dozen elderflowers. Repeat for remaining portions.

HONEYSUCKLE-POACHED RHUBARB, ICE CREAM, KNOTWEED JAM, LOVAGE GRANITE

When honeysuckle flowers in late May, we take as much as we can get our hands on. That season is as fleeting as the flower's floral, honeyed flavor. To capture it we make tons of honeysuckle simple syrup to use as a poaching vehicle for months to come. (If you only make one component from this recipe, make the syrup; it's fantastic as a sweetener for lemonade, iced tea, cocktails, and seltzer.) For our spring tasting dessert, we poach rhubarb in the honeysuckle syrup, then pair it with jam made from knotweed, an invasive plant with an acidity that mimics rhubarb's. To balance the sweet-tart profile, we add a gorgeous lovage granite, which brings a refreshing herbal quality. Fat in the form of raw-milk ice cream rounds it all out.

We process the ice cream in our Pacojet, but the same base will work in a standard electric ice cream maker. Raw milk is best for this recipe because of its full flavor and high fat content, but if you're in one of the states that outlaws unpasteurized dairy, you can substitute pasteurized as long as it's full-fat and, ideally, from grass-fed cows.

MAKES 6 PORTIONS

ICE CREAM

3.5 ounces/100 g granulated sugar
1.7 ounces/50 g glucose syrup
1.6 ounces/48 g milk powder
10.5 ounces/300 g raw heavy whipping cream
17 ounces/500 g raw milk
1 tablespoon/10 g Cremodan 30

Purée all the ingredients together in a blender, and transfer to a medium pot. Warm the mixture over medium-low heat to 185°F. Cool. Purée again, and pack the mixture into 2 Pacojet containers. Freeze overnight. Process for at least an hour before serving, and reserve frozen.

LOVAGE GRANITE

3 ounces/85 g granulated sugar
8 ounces/226 g lovage leaves
.9 ounce/25 g confectioners' sugar
7 ounces/207 g water
Pinch of Kosher salt

Combine all the ingredients in a blender, and blend on high until very smooth. Pass the purée through a chinois into a shallow pan, and place in the freezer. Scrape the mixture with a fork every 20 minutes until it is icy and fluffy. Cover and reserve frozen.

KNOTWEED JAM

1 pound/454 g knotweed, sliced into ¼-inch/6-cm pieces
.6 ounce/17 g pectin
1 pound/454 g granulated sugar

Place the knotweed slices in a medium pot, and add enough water to barely submerge. Bring to a simmer and cook for 5 minutes. Smash the knotweed while it's still warm with a potato masher, and strain through a chinois lined with a coffee filter. Place the strained liquid in a medium pot, whisk in the pectin, and simmer for 2 minutes. Whisk in the sugar in thirds, then bring to a boil. Boil for 2 minutes. Drop a small amount of the jam on a cold plate to test the gelling. If the liquid sets up immediately, the jam is ready; if not, allow it to reduce 5 more minutes and test again. Store in a nonreactive airtight container in the refrigerator for up to 3 weeks.

POACHED RHUBARB

3 ounces/85 g granulated sugar
1 ounce/28 g honeysuckle flowers
3 ounces/90 g water
2 stalks rhubarb

Set a circulator to 145°F. Bring the sugar, honeysuckle, and water to a simmer in a small pot. Stir to dissolve the sugar, then cool, and strain. Cut the tips off the rhubarb, and peel off the red skin. Cut the rhubarb into 4-inch/10-cm pieces, and place in a medium vacuum bag with the honeysuckle syrup. Seal on high, and poach the rhubarb sous vide for 45 minutes. Reserve cold.

TO PLATE

Olio Verde

Set a 3.2-inch/8-cm ring mold in a bowl. Fill one side of the mold (to the halfway point) with poached rhubarb and 1 tablespoon/35 g knotweed jam. Fill the other half with ½ cup/100 g ice cream, smoothing the surface with the back of a warm spoon. Garnish the ice cream with a few drops of Olio Verde. Remove the ring mold, and cover the exposed rhubarb and jam with the granite. Repeat for the remaining portions, and serve immediately.

COCKTAIL: A BIRD NAMED BARB

Our kitchen and our bar are in constant communication. Take this rhubarb-centric Bird Named Barb, a riff on the Jungle Bird, a tiki classic made with Campari, rum, pineapple, simple syrup, and lime. We had a great rhubarb season last year and made lots of rhubarb vinegar, which we turned into a delicious pale pink shrub. Where you would typically use mild white wine or cider vinegar in a shrub, ours has that rhubarb vinegar foundation, giving it double-strength flavor. Here, the shrub replaces the pineapple juice in the Jungle Bird recipe. Gin replaces rum. Honey syrup brings a more complex sweetness than simple syrup. Sfumato Rabarbaro, a dark, smoky amaro that counts rhubarb among its ingredients, cuts the intensity of the Campari. This shaken drink is strained into a tall Baccarat crystal Collins glass—when Chef Perrier downsized recently, he gave us his collection from Le Bec—and topped with crushed ice and a metal straw. Definitely a cocktail that looks as good as it tastes.

MAKES 1 COCKTAIL

RHUBARB SHRUB

1 pound/454 g rhubarb, chopped
⅓ pound/150 g sugar
Rhubarb Vinegar (see page 159)

Combine the rhubarb and sugar in a container, and macerate overnight in the refrigerator. Transfer the mixture to a saucepan, and cook over low heat until the rhubarb is soft, about 15 minutes. Cool and purée. Weigh the purée. Measure out ⅓ of the weight of the purée in rhubarb vinegar. Whisk the vinegar into the purée, transfer it to a quart container, and reserve chilled.

HONEY SYRUP

17.7 ounces/500 g honey
8.7 ounces/250 g hot water

Put the honey in a quart container and carefully pour the water over it. Stir until the honey is melted. Cover and reserve chilled.

1½ ounces/44.3 ml London dry gin
¼ ounce/7.4 ml Sfumato Rabarbaro amaro
¼ ounce/7.4 ml Campari
1 ounce/29.6 ml Rhubarb Shrub
1 ounce/29.6 ml Honey Syrup
½ ounce/14.7 ml lime juice

Place all the ingredients in a shaker. Fill the shaker halfway with ice, and shake for 5 seconds. Strain into a Collins glass, and top with crushed ice. Serve with a metal straw.

Tonight We Are Serving

I.
Marigold-Compressed Kohlrabi,
Buckwheat Honey, Cured Egg

II.
Green Tomato Confit, Green Gooseberry,
Green Coriander, Almond

III.
Paddlefish Caviar, Vodka Cream,
Salsify Ice Cream

IV.
Maine Mussels, Zucchini, Saffron

V.
Blue Crab Porridge, Soft-Shell Custard,
Hickory Nuts

VI.
Sea Robin, Apricot, Chanterelles

VII.
Grilled Quail, Black Garlic Scape, Cherries

VIII.
Pork Cheek, Blueberry Miso, Crispy Pork Granola

IX.
White Chocolate Pudding,
Cocoa Crumble, Strawberries

X.
Cocktail: Rum, Johnnie, Rum

MARIGOLD-COMPRESSED KOHLRABI, BUCKWHEAT HONEY, CURED EGG

I've been infatuated with kohlrabi from when I first tasted it as a twenty-three-year-old cook. I was having dinner at Wallsé, a fine-dining Austrian restaurant in New York, where they served kohlrabi with radishes and fish. I had no idea what kohlrabi was, and the server described it to me as a sweet turnip, which is a pretty fair comparison. I don't know why kohlrabi isn't more popular. It's crunchy and gorgeous and the entire thing is edible up the leaves, which are great braised. Here we highlight the cool, crunchy bulb of the vegetable in a snack designed to combat the South Philly summer, a season as hot and sticky as a stack of pancakes. We compress the kohlrabi in a saffron-colored syrup steeped with marigold, another one of those microseason ingredients (see Honeysuckle-Poached Rhubarb, page 116) that we batch up for the kitchen and the bar. The marigold syrup has this really cool candied-orange flavor that works so well with the kohlrabi, which has a natural affinity for citrus. It's nice to be able to give guests something that will cool them down right after they arrive, sometimes after walking a couple of blocks from a distant parking spot; South Philly is wonderful in many ways, but parking ain't one of them.

CURED EGGS

2 cups/450 g white miso
1 cup/225 g Kosher salt
⅓ cup/79 ml water
Yolks from 6 extra-large eggs

Pulse the miso, salt, and water in a food processor until smooth. Pour a layer of the miso cure in a shallow, nonreactive airtight container. Carefully place the yolks on top of the cure. Spoon the remaining cure over the top of the yolks, and refrigerate for 2 days. Rinse the yolks in cold water, and dry in a dehydrator at 130°F for 12 hours or until hard. Reserve in a cool, dry place.

MARIGOLD-COMPRESSED KOHLRABI

14 ounces/400 g granulated sugar
14 ounces/400 g verjus
20 ounces/600 g water
2 ounces/60 g marigold flowers
1 kohlrabi bulb

Bring the sugar, verjus, and water up to a simmer, stirring to dissolve the sugar. Place the marigolds in a nonreactive airtight container. Pour the verjus mixture over the marigolds and cover. Steep overnight in the refrigerator. Strain out and discard the marigolds, and reserve the syrup at room temperature. Use a vegetable sheeter to roll out the kohlrabi into four 9 x ¾-inch/23 x 2-cm strips. Place the strips flat in a medium vacuum bag with 2 tablespoons/30 g of the syrup. Seal on high. Rest for 3 hours in the refrigerator.

BUCKWHEAT HONEY GEL

4.9 ounces/140 g buckwheat honey
⅓ cup/79 ml water
1 teaspoon/2 g agar-agar

Slowly bring the honey to a boil in a high-sided pot, cooking it until it becomes very dark, about 4 minutes. Slowly deglaze the pot with water; the mixture will boil up, so be careful. Remove from the heat and strain. Weigh out the liquid. It should measure 6 to 7 ounces/150 to 200 g. Whisk in the agar, return the liquid to a pot, and bring it to a simmer. Transfer the gel to a pan, cool, and allow it to set in the fridge, about 1 hour. Purée until smooth, and reserve cold in a plastic squeeze bottle.

TO PLATE

Black Lime Powder (see page 162)
4 borage leaves

Tightly roll each strip of kohlrabi into a cigar shape. Grate the cured yolks on a rasp grater into a shallow dish. Dip one end of each kohlrabi roll into the grated egg. Stand the rolls on serving plates, egg-side up, 2 rolls per plate. Top each roll with a dot of buckwheat honey gel, and dust with black lime powder. Garnish each roll with a borage leaf.

GREEN TOMATO CONFIT, GREEN GOOSEBERRY, GREEN CORIANDER, ALMOND

The real name for this dish is Chill, Everybody, It's Not Tomato Season Yet. As soon as the weather warms up here, everyone is like, "Ooh! Tomatoes!" But they don't hit their sweetest peak until the end of August, pushing September. So the idea for this dish came from playing off that premature rush with a cast of three green (unripe) ingredients: gooseberries, coriander, and, of course, tomatoes.

Green tomatoes are right in my wheelhouse: very fruity but unbelievably acidic. Working on this dish, it was fun experimenting with ways to round out that big personality. We settled on two preparations of tomato: an unctuous confit topped with a smooth gelée that coats your tongue. It's vibrant instead of aggressively sour, and the texture messes with your mind—green tomatoes are supposed to be crunchy and sharp, not lush and almost fatty. We reintroduce acid to the dish with fermented green gooseberries and pickled green coriander, another specialty of Green Meadow Farm. I'm not a complete cilantro hater, but it's not my favorite flavor. Green coriander—the tiny young seed clusters that appear after a cilantro plant has flowered—I love. The flavor is grassy and herbal, nutty and citrusy, and pickling only amplifies it. I eat this dish just to chase those seeds, each one a quick kick of coriander flavor.

MAKES 4 PORTIONS

PICKLED GREEN CORIANDER

1 bunch green coriander
9 ounces/266 g water
6 ounces/177 g verjus
3 ounces/88 g granulated sugar

Pick the green coriander seeds from the stems, and place them in a small vacuum bag. Bring the water, verjus, and sugar to a simmer, stirring to dissolve the sugar. Cool completely. Pour the liquid over the coriander, seal the bag on high, and refrigerate for 3 weeks.

FERMENTED GOOSEBERRIES

1 pound/454 g green (unripe) gooseberries
.5 ounce/15 g Kosher salt
1 sprig tarragon

Toss all the ingredients together, and place them in a large vacuum bag. Seal on high, and leave in a cool, dry place until the bag puffs, about 1 week. Reserve cold.

GREEN TOMATO GELÉE

6 green (unripe) tomatoes
Grated zest and juice of 2 sudachi
1 tablespoon/15 g koji extract
Kosher salt
¼ teaspoon/.5 g agar-agar
3.5 sheets silver gelatin

Juice the tomatoes, and measure out 1 pint/500 g, reserving the excess for another use. Add the sudachi zest and juice and the koji extract. Stir and adjust the seasoning with salt if necessary. Whisk together 3.75 ounces/100 g of the seasoned juice with the agar in a small pot, and simmer for 2 minutes. Temper the hot mixture into the rest of the juice. Transfer the mixture to a shallow pan, and allow it to set in the refrigerator for 2 hours. Slowly pass it through 3 layers of cheesecloth to clarify. This should produce about 1 pint/500 g of strained clear juice left over.

Soften the gelatin in ice water. Squeeze out any excess water, and place the gelatin in a small pot with 3.75 ounces/100 g of the strained clear juice, reserving the rest of the juice. Warm until the gelatin has melted, and emulsify into the reserved juice with a whisk. Transfer the gel to a pan, and allow it to set for 3 hours in the refrigerator.

ALMOND MILK PURÉE

1 cup/225 g blanched almonds
14 ounces/414 g water
1 teaspoon/5 g Kosher salt
1¼ teaspoons/3.5 g agar-agar

Purée the almonds with the water in a blender on high for 5 minutes, and strain through a chinois. Reserve the liquid and discard the solids. Season the liquid with the salt. Measure out 11 ounces/350 g of liquid. Combine the liquid and the agar-agar in a small pot, and simmer for 2 minutes. Transfer to a pan and

cool in the refrigerator until set, about 2 hours. Purée until smooth, transfer to a plastic squeeze bottle, and reserve cold.

GREEN TOMATO CONFIT

2 large green (unripe) tomatoes
1 teaspoon/5 g Kosher salt
1 tablespoon/15 g extra-virgin olive oil
1 sprig lemon verbena
1 sprig tarragon

Set a circulator to 160°F. Cut the green tomatoes in half from top to bottom. Season lightly with the salt, and transfer to a small vacuum bag with the olive oil and herbs. Seal on high, and cook sous vide for 35 minutes. Cool in an ice bath. Cut the tomatoes into ¼-inch/7-mm slices, then trim them into 2-inch/5-cm bars. Reserve cold.

TO PLATE

Set 2 bars of confit tomato in the bottom of a bowl, and cover half the confit with 1 tablespoon/15 g green tomato gelée. Place 3 dots of almond milk purée on the uncovered portion of the confit. Garnish all over with 8 thin slices of fermented gooseberry and 10 green coriander buds. Repeat for remaining portions.

PADDLEFISH CAVIAR, VODKA CREAM, SALSIFY ICE CREAM

Six years in at Laurel, we're fortunate to have many regulars. Our approach to hospitality is individualized, so when someone comes in for dinner, then comes again three weeks later, we want to make sure they're getting a different meal even though the menu may not have changed in a significant way. This is why we keep some extra-special ingredients on hand, like caviar. Along with our pickle and preserve larder, they allow us to create dishes on the fly that we can pop into a tasting as a substitution or bonus course. That's how this plate came about. We had paddlefish in stock and some salsify ice cream kicking around the kitchen from another dish we were working on, and I remembered a recipe in Chef Perrier's cookbook for *les oeufs surprise au caviar*, a hollowed egg filled with vodka cream and topped with caviar. We made a vodka whipped cream flavored with chives, lemon, and sieved egg, formed it into a quenelle, and plated it with matching quenelles of caviar and salsify ice cream, all the scoops touching at the center of the plate like a three-tipped black-and-white star. In most of our dishes we aim to hit sour, sweet, salty, and bitter, but sometimes we instead go with a single, really strong note. Here you have one salty element, one creamy element, and one salty-and-creamy element. When you get a little bit of each quenelle together on a spoon, the rush of salinity and fat, followed by a glimmer of sweetness, is a total knockout.

SALSIFY ICE CREAM

2 lemons, halved
3 pounds/1.4 kg salsify
Kosher salt
6.5 cups/1,500 g heavy whipping cream
20 ounces/570 g granulated sugar
¼ teaspoon/.7 g xanthan gum

Before peeling the salsify, squeeze the juice from the lemons into a large pot of cold water, and add the squeezed rinds. As you peel the salsify, place the peeled pieces in the lemon water to prevent oxidation. Juice the salsify, weigh the juice, and add 2.5 percent of the weight in salt. Transfer the juice to a large vacuum bag, seal on high, and leave it in a cool, dry place for 2 weeks.

Strain the fermented salsify juice. Weigh out 25.6 ounces/750 g of the juice, and add it to a blender with the cream, sugar, and 1 teaspoon/5 g salt. Purée on low while adding the xanthan. Freeze the ice cream base in 2 Pacojet containers, and process the following day an hour before serving. Reserve frozen.

VODKA CREAM

3 eggs
1 pint/473 g heavy whipping cream
2 tablespoons/29 g vodka
Juice of 2 lemons
¼ bunch chives, minced
1 teaspoon/5 g Kosher salt

Place the eggs in a small pot and cover with water. Bring to a simmer, cover with a tight-fitting lid, and remove from the heat. After 10 minutes crack the eggs lightly, and rinse them in ice water. Peel the eggs, and separate the yolks from the whites. Pass the whites and the yolks separately through a fine sieve, and reserve cold.

Whip the cream until stiff. Soften the cream with the vodka and lemon juice. Gently fold in the sieved eggs, chives, and salt. Reserve cold.

TO PLATE

8 ounces/256 g paddlefish caviar

Freeze 8 plates at least an hour before serving. Quickly form and place a quenelle each of caviar, ice cream, and vodka cream on each plate. Serve immediately.

MAINE MUSSELS, ZUCCHINI, SAFFRON

There's nothing wrong with mussels steamed in tomato sauce or white wine and garlic, which is what most of us think of when we think about mussels. But in a fine-dining context, I think they're an underappreciated protein. You can take that mild mussel flavor and intensify it, which is what we do here by turning two pounds of steamed Maine bivalves into a nimble saffron-scented broth and a rich, slightly tangy purée that's pretty much mussel mayo. We tuck a couple of steamed mussel meats in there and top the dish with green and gold ribbons of different varieties of zucchini and summer squash, which are in abundance in the area by July. Salting the raw squashes ahead of time breaks down their cellular structure and makes them pliable, so by the time the warm broth hits them, you're getting a half-cooked vegetable that's softened but still maintains a snap. It's a terrific complement to the brininess of the mussels, the fat of the purée, and the brightness of the broth.

MAKES 4 PORTIONS

MUSSELS

2 tablespoons/30 g grapeseed oil
1 white onion, sliced
2 sprigs thyme
1 bay leaf
2 pounds/900 g Maine mussels, rinsed and
    debearded

Heat a large pot with a tight-fitting lid until it's very hot. Add the oil to the pot, then quickly add the onion, thyme, and bay leaf, and cook until caramelized, about 6 minutes. Add the mussels and cover. Steam for 2 to 5 minutes or until the mussels just open. Strain the mussels, reserving the liquid, and cool the mussels on a sheet pan in the refrigerator. The reserved liquid will measure about 1 pint/500 g; if necessary, top it off with water to reach that volume. Remove the meat from the mussels, discarding the shells, and reserve at room temperature for the mussel purée and for plating.

MUSSEL BROTH

1 tablespoon/15 g grapeseed oil
½ bulb fennel, sliced
3 shallots, sliced
½ white onion, sliced
2 sprigs thyme
1 cup/250 g Chablis
1 teaspoon/2 g saffron threads
1 pint/500 g reserved mussel liquid
1½ teaspoons/4 g xanthan gum

Place the oil, fennel, shallots, onion, and thyme in a medium pot. Caramelize well over medium heat, about 6 minutes. Deglaze the pot with the wine, and reduce until evaporated. Add the saffron and the reserved mussel liquid, and reduce by half. Strain and reduce by half. Add the xanthan, and emulsify with an immersion blender for 2 minutes. Reserve warm.

MUSSEL PURÉE

2 tablespoons/30 g Champagne vinegar
3 egg yolks
1 cup/225 g grapeseed oil
1.8 ounces/50 g reserved shelled mussels
Kosher salt

Purée the vinegar and the egg yolks in a blender until thick. With the blender running on low, slowly stream the oil into the mixture. Adjust with ice water as necessary until the emulsion reaches a mayonnaise consistency. Purée in the mussels, and adjust the seasoning with salt as needed. Pass through a sieve, and reserve in a plastic squeeze bottle at room temperature.

TO PLATE

8 very thin lengthwise slices green zucchini
8 very thin lengthwise slices grey zucchini
8 very thin lengthwise slices yellow squash
Kosher salt
12 reserved shelled mussels
1 tablespoon/15 g unsalted butter
32 leaves lime balm

Lay out the squash slices on a sheet pan. Sprinkle salt over the slices, and allow to soften for 10 minutes.

Meanwhile, very gently warm the mussels in the butter. Transfer the mussels to a paper towel to absorb excess grease. Set out 4 steep-sided bowls, and put a large dollop of the mussel purée in the bottom of each. Place 3 mussels on top of the purée in each bowl. Arrange the squash slices over the mussels. Garnish each portion with 8 leaves of lime balm. Spoon the broth over each portion tableside.

BLUE CRAB PORRIDGE, SOFT-SHELL CUSTARD, HICKORY NUTS

"For your fish course this evening, you have tuna with melon and carrot," a server at a New York restaurant said, setting down a one-by-one-inch cube of tuna in front of my wife and me. Kristen laughed, literally out loud, and at the end of the meal (which she dubbed a three-hour hors d'oeuvre party) we went out for sushi because we were so hungry. I never want a guest to feel that way at Laurel. Even in the summer, when we keep the menu relatively light, with an emphasis on cold dishes and vegetables, we still want our guests to feel like they got fed, not like they need a pizza after dinner. So the question we ask is, how do we achieve that without beating people over the head with pasta or gigantic pieces of protein? This crab porridge is a neat solution. The flavor of blue crabs has profound depth but is also very light on its feet, making it an ideal feature midway through the summer tasting. We spin soft-shells into custard, turn blue bodies into broth, and fold sweet white crabmeat into a savory porridge of al dente grains, seeds, and nuts. Plated together with a refreshing herb purée and bronze fennel, it hits that Goldilocks zone of not too heavy and not too delicate, exactly what we're looking for as we begin to build to the menu's climax.

MAKES 4 PORTIONS

GRAINS

½ cup/90 g black barley
2 quarts/2 L water, divided
2 tablespoons/30 g Kosher salt, divided
½ cup/80 g black quinoa
¼ cup/45 g hickory nuts

Preheat the oven to 325°F. Place the barley in a china cap and rinse well. Transfer to a medium pot with half the water, and bring to a simmer, adding more water if needed. Season with half the salt, and cook slowly for 45 minutes or until tender. Strain and cool on a sheet pan. Repeat the process with the quinoa, remaining water, and remaining salt, cooking for 25 minutes. Strain and cool on a sheet pan.

Toast the hickory nuts in the oven for 8 minutes, tossing halfway through, and reserve at room temperature.

CRAB BROTH

4 hard-shell blue crabs, cleaned and halved
1 white carrot, sliced
2 shallots, sliced
1 leek, sliced
1 cup/250 g Chablis
4 quarts/4 L water
Kosher salt

Roughly chop the crabs, and place them in the bowl of a pressure cooker with the vegetables and wine. Simmer over high heat until the wine is reduced by half. Add the water and lock the lid. Cook on high pressure for 30 minutes. Strain the broth and reduce by half. Adjust the seasoning with salt as needed.

SOFT-SHELL CRAB CUSTARD

Butter, for greasing
1 pint/500 g whole milk
13.3 ounces/400 g heavy whipping cream
2 soft-shell crabs ("whales")
4 egg yolks
Kosher salt

Preheat the oven to 325°F. Lightly butter a 13 x 7-inch/33 x 18-cm baking pan. Boil a kettle of water.

Combine the milk and the cream in a medium pot, and bring to a simmer. Remove the gills from the crabs. In a blender, combine the egg yolks and the crabs, and purée on high speed until smooth. Reduce the speed, and slowly temper in the hot milk and cream mixture. Season with salt. Pass the custard base through a chinois, and pour it into the buttered pan. Bake in a hot water bath in the oven for 25 to 35 minutes or until just set. Reserve warm.

TO PLATE

¼ cup/45 g sunflower seeds
2 tablespoons / 30 g unsalted butter
6 ounces/180 g blue crab meat
1 tablespoon/3 g finely minced chives
1 tablespoon/5 g chiffonade of parsley
1 teaspoon/5 g Kosher salt
4 tablespoons/25 g Herb Purée (see page 164)
Bronze fennel fronds

To make the porridge, place the sunflower seeds, toasted hickory nuts, and 4 tablespoons/60 g each of the cooked barley and quinoa in a medium pot. Cover with 3 ounces/85 g crab broth, and bring to a simmer over medium heat. Fold in the butter, crab meat, chives, parsley, and salt.

Form 1 tablespoon/6 g herb purée into a quenelle, and set it in the bottom of a bowl. Form 1 tablespoon/6 g warm custard into a quenelle, and place it next to the herb purée. Garnish with bronze fennel fronds. Spoon one-fourth of the porridge into the bowl. Repeat for remaining portions.

SEA ROBIN, APRICOT, CHANTERELLES

A couple of years ago we did a crudo series with our seafood purveyor, Samuels & Son. They'd send us different bycatch every week: triggerfish, gurnard, tautog—the "trash" species that are often thrown back into the ocean. It's important for us to show that these fish can be delicious when treated correctly; otherwise we're just helping to deplete the stocks of wild striped bass, fluke, and other, more popular species that swim around here. This is how I was introduced to sea robin, a bottom dweller with big jaws for chewing on crabs, mussels, and clams. Fishermen in Jersey have told me that sea robins are not good eating, but I totally disagree. The concentration of iodine in its diet makes its flesh sweet. You have to cook sea robin delicately, though, to avoid making it tough and stringy. For us, that means a two-hour cure followed by thirty-five minutes at a low temperature in a CVap, a humidity-controlled oven that cooks with wet heat. This ensures that the sea robin stays moist. If you don't have a CVap, use a regular oven set to 200°F. The main downside to sea robin is its low yield, only about 25 percent, which is why you need two fish to get the four small servings this recipe calls for. Use the scraps and skeletons to make a superior fish stock.

As with our Black Trumpet Mushroom–Stuffed Dover Sole (page 72), we include mushrooms to complement the robin. I really like how their earthiness pairs with fish. We ferment chanterelles and shiitakes and separate out the liquid, which becomes the foundation of the crème fraîche–thickened sauce. The solids are dehydrated into a powder seasoned with lemon and miso. Fresh chanterelles and morels sautéed with butter and kombu join the robin on the pickup. Look for very young mushrooms for this component; they have a natural acidity that, with the apricot gel, works to brighten the dish.

MAKES 4 PORTIONS

MUSHROOM SAUCE AND FISH SEASONING

1.7 pounds/750 g shiitake mushrooms

8.8 ounces/250 g chanterelle mushrooms

.8 ounces/25 g Kosher salt

1 tablespoon/20 g crème fraîche

2 tablespoons/15 g vin jaune

2 tablespoons/20 g Fermented Black Trumpet Powder (see page 162)

2 tablespoons/28 g lemon powder

2 tablespoons/28 g miso powder

Purée the mushrooms and salt together in a food processor. Transfer to a medium vacuum bag and seal on high. Reserve in a cool, dry place for 1 week. Strain out the liquid, reserving both the liquid and the solids. Bring the liquid to a simmer with the crème fraîche. Stir in the vin jaune, cool to room temperature, and reserve cold.

Dehydrate the mushroom solids at 125°F until completely dry, about 6 hours. Grind into a powder, and measure out 2 tablespoons/20 g. Combine with the black trumpet, lemon, and miso powders. Reserve at room temperature in a mesh-top shaker.

SEA ROBIN

2 whole sea robins, 1.5 to 2 pounds/680 to 907 g
 each, or 4 2-ounce/57-g fillets
2 large sheets kombu
Kosher salt
4 cardamom leaves

Fillet the fish, and remove the skin and the pin bones. Rinse the sheets of kombu under warm water until pliable. Shake dry. Lay the fillets over 1 sheet of kombu, and place the second sheet of kombu over the top. Cure in the refrigerator for 2 hours. Remove the fillets from the kombu leaves. Lightly season them with salt. Wrap the fillets in cardamom leaves and reserve cold.

APRICOT GEL

1 cup/250 g apricot vinegar
1 teaspoon/2.75 g agar-agar
.5 ounce/15 g glucose syrup

Combine the vinegar, agar, and glucose in a small pot and bring to a simmer. Remove from the heat and allow to set. Purée the mixture until smooth, and pass through a sieve. Transfer to a plastic squeeze bottle and reserve cold.

TO PLATE

4 ounces/115 g chanterelles
4 ounces/115 g morels
2 tablespoons/30 g unsalted butter
1 small piece kombu
20 pieces Salty Fingers
20 broccoli rabe flowers

Set a CVap oven to 122°F with 80 percent humidity. Place the cardamom leaf–wrapped sea robin fillets in the oven for 35 minutes.

While the fish is cooking, warm the mushroom sauce over low heat. Gently wash the mushrooms in lukewarm water and pat dry. Quarter the chanterelles and slice the morels. Warm the butter in a medium pot, and add the mushrooms and kombu. Stir well, and slowly cook over low heat until the mushrooms are tender but still firm, about 2 minutes.

Once the fish is cooked, remove the cardamom leaves and generously dust the fillets with the mushroom powder. Place 1 portion in the center of a bowl. Add a few drops of apricot gel and 3 slices each of chanterelle and morel. Garnish with 5 Salty Fingers and 5 broccoli rabe flowers. Repeat for remaining portions. Aerate the mushroom sauce with an immersion blender until frothy, and spoon alongside each portion.

GRILLED QUAIL, BLACK GARLIC SCAPE, CHERRIES

As my wife and I get older, we're trying to take better care of our bodies, and that means that many of our dinners at home—where Kristen does most of the cooking—feature proteins and vegetables cooked on our grill. Not fancy or cheffy, just simple stuff like sweet potatoes, chicken, fish. I can't even say we start grilling when the weather gets nice. We start grilling as soon as the snow stops. This cherry-glazed grilled quail isn't something we make at home, but it takes its inspiration from barbecue-sauced chicken you might have at a backyard cookout. The glaze, which we make with cherries and vinegar spiced with cardamom and grains of paradise, is sweet and sticky. The quail is smoky not just from the Japanese charcoal we grill it over, but also from toasty genmaicha tea steeped in the brine. You'll want to pick it up and eat it with your hands.

MAKES 4 PORTIONS

BLACK GARLIC SCAPES

1 pound/454 g garlic scapes

Rinse and dry the scapes. Place them in a large vacuum bag and seal on high. Put the bagged scapes in a dehydrator, and dehydrate at 125°F for 3 weeks or until black. Remove the scapes from the bag and reserve cold.

QUAIL

1 quart/1 L water
2 ounces/57 g Kosher salt
1.75 ounces/50 g genmaicha tea
2 whole quail, 8 ounces/227 g each

Warm the water to 160°F in a medium pot. Add the salt and genmaicha and steep for 5 minutes. Strain the liquid and cool it to room temperature; reserve cold.

Separate the legs from the quail. Pour the brine over the legs and cages and reserve cold for 6 hours. Drain the quail and pat dry. Air dry for 12 hours, uncovered, in the fridge.

CHERRY GLAZE

1 pound/454 g pitted Bing cherries
1 tablespoon/10 g grains of paradise
2 green cardamom pods, cracked
1 ounce/28 g red wine vinegar

Juice the cherries and strain the juice. Reserve the juice and discard all solids.

Toast the grains of paradise and cardamom over low heat in a small dry skillet until fragrant, about 5 minutes. Combine the toasted spices, cherry juice, and vinegar in a medium pot and reduce by half over medium-high heat. Strain, and reduce again until thick and shiny. Reserve at room temperature.

TO PLATE

4 baby leeks

2 tablespoons/60 g brown butter

Maldon sea salt

4 Bing cherries, quartered

4 Rainier cherries, quartered

4 ounces/112 g Quail Jus (see page 157), warmed

Get a grill hot. Grill the quail cages over direct heat, continually rotating them to crisp the skin while brushing with the cherry glaze, for 20 minutes or until the meat registers 132°F on an instant-read thermometer. Remove the cages from the grill and rest for 10 minutes. While the cages are resting, place the quail legs on the grill. Cook the legs for 4 minutes per side, brushing with the glaze before and after flipping. Remove the legs from the grill and rest for 3 minutes.

Meanwhile, cook the leeks in the brown butter in a medium pot over low heat for 2 minutes. Slice each leek in half lengthwise.

Cut the breasts off the cages, and cut each breast in half crossways. Sprinkle the cut sides of each breast piece with sea salt. Set out 4 plates. Place 2 halves of a breast and 1 leg in the center of each plate. Divide the cherries and leeks among the plates. Garnish each plate with 1 garlic scape and 1 ounce/28 g quail jus.

PORK CHEEK, BLUEBERRY MISO, CRISPY PORK GRANOLA

We've played with several different techniques for cooking pork cheeks, but this process, which mimics the one for preparing corned beef, is our favorite. We brine the pork for four days, then cook it sous vide for thirty-six hours. The texture produced isn't like a falling-apart-soft braised meat. Yes, the cheek is tender and delicate, but you've still got to cut at it a little. On the pickup, we sear it, warm it through, glaze it in a pot of really dark, intense pork sauce, and press one side into a pile of crispy pork "granola." (Use the leftover granola to garnish salads, vegetable dishes, pasta—basically anywhere you want salt and crunch.) Sauce-side up, the cheek looks almost black on the plate, but then you slice it to reveal this rosy pink interior, an unexpected surprise. You can achieve similar results with pork belly and shoulder, if cheeks aren't available.

The pork cheek represents the largest concentration of umami, fat, and salt in the summer tasting. As the last stop on the menu before dessert, that's intentional, but we also want to keep those flavors in check. Enter the blueberry miso. Pork with summer fruit—cherries, peaches, apricots—is a classic combination, but I'd argue that the meat tastes best with blueberries. South Jersey is home to a huge blueberry industry, and the season runs all the way from June through August. For this dish, we cure blueberries in miso and purée them into a condiment that's very sweet and acidic with a subtly funky undertone. This recipe, incidentally, would be great with pitted cherries, peaches, or apricots, so feel free to experiment with pairing different fruit misos with this pork cheek or other proteins.

MAKES 4 PORTIONS

BLUEBERRY MISO

2 pints/900 g blueberries
8 ounces/240 g white miso
4 ounces/112 g Kosher salt
2 ounces/56 g granulated sugar
4 ounces/113.4 g water

Rinse the blueberries well and discard any that are bruised. Mix the miso, salt, sugar, and water in a bowl until smooth. Gently fold in the blueberries. Transfer the mix to a nonreactive airtight container, and store in a cool, dry place for 1 week. Remove the blueberries from the miso and rinse well. Purée one-third of the blueberries in a blender, pass the purée through a chinois, and reserve cold in a plastic squeeze bottle. Reserve the remaining whole blueberries cold.

PORK CHEEKS

4 pork cheeks, about 4 ounces/113 g each
1 quart/1 L Meat Brine (see page 158)

Clean the cheeks by removing any outer fat and sinew, and rinse well. Place the cheeks and the brine in a large vacuum bag, seal on high, and reserve in the refrigerator for 4 days. Set a circulator to 147°F. Cook the cheeks sous vide for 36 hours. Remove the bag from the water bath and reserve it at room temperature for 1 hour. Chill the bag in an ice bath for 1 hour. Reserve in the refrigerator for at least 1 day but no more than 1 week.

CRISPY PORK GRANOLA

2 pounds/900 g pig ear
13 ounces/370 g Kosher salt, divided
2 quarts/2 L canola oil

Rinse the ears well and remove or burn off any hair with a crème brûlée torch. Place the ears in a stockpot and cover with water. Bring to a strong boil then remove from the heat. Strain and rinse the ears. Return the ears to a fresh pot and cover with water. Season the water with 12 ounces/340 g of the salt. Simmer the ears until tender, about 2 hours and 15 minutes. Strain the ears and cool completely.

Once the ears are cool and firm, grind them in a meat grinder fitted with the fine-die attachment. Dehydrate the ground ears at 140°F for 14 hours or until very dry and firm.

Bring the canola oil to 375°F in a stockpot. In 3 batches, fry the dehydrated pork, which will lightly puff and turn golden-brown in color. Drain the fried pork on a sheet pan lined with paper towels, and season with the remaining salt. Reserve in a nonreactive airtight container in a cool, dry place.

TO PLATE

1 tablespoon/15 g unsalted butter
1 tablespoon/15 g grapeseed oil
12 reserved blueberries
1 cup Pork Jus (see page 157)
Grated zest of 1 lemon
Grated zest of 1 lime
Minced chives
4 ounces/115 g julienned celtuce
1 teaspoon salt

Preheat the oven to 200°F. Melt the butter and oil together in a cast-iron pan. Sear the pork cheeks over high heat until golden-brown, about 2 minutes per side, continually basting with the fat. Transfer the cheeks to the oven to warm through for about 20 minutes, or until an instant-read thermometer inserted into the meat registers 150°F. At the same time, place the reserved blueberries in the oven in a separate pot. Remove the berries when you remove the pork cheeks.

Transfer the cheeks to a pot and cover them with pork jus. Bring to a simmer, glazing until the jus sticks well to the meat.

Toss the celtuce with the salt and rest for 10 minutes. Rinse and pat try.

Fill a shallow dish with the pork granola, and stir in the citrus zests and chives. Dip one side of each cheek into the granola. Set each cheek on a plate. Add a quenelle of blueberry miso purée and pile of celtuce to each plate. Garnish each portion with 3 of the reserved blueberries and a drizzle of the pork jus.

WHITE CHOCOLATE PUDDING, COCOA CRUMBLE, STRAWBERRIES

I'm not a fan of white chocolate. But I love caramelized white chocolate, which has a whole other flavor profile. It's been following me around since 2012. At Rittenhouse Tavern, it came in the form of a frozen caramelized white chocolate panna cotta. On the finale of my season of *Top Chef*, in Hawaii, it evolved into a pudding set with agar and jeweled with tropical fruits. When we opened Laurel, it was one of the first desserts to go on the menu (back when we had an à la carte menu), not just because it's delicious but because of our kitchen constraints. We don't have the space to pre-plate thirty desserts, chill them in the fridge, and garnish them à la minute. (We don't have the space to do that for even ten desserts.) So we calibrated the balance of custard to chocolate to create a pudding that will hold its texture in a pastry bag, one that we constantly pull in and out of the fridge to pipe out desserts to order.

The order of this recipe is important. Sometimes strawberry season here is as short as two weeks, so we make as many different strawberry things for as long as we can. The various strawberry garnishes can be prepped in advance, as can the super easy chocolate crumble you will want to put over everything from now on. But when you're ready for the pudding, dial up your concentration and get all the ingredients mise-d out before you start. The process goes fast, and you have to monitor the temperatures of the chocolate and the custard. If the former gets too cool, it will seize up. If the latter gets too hot, the sugar will turn it into a brick. You should be caramelizing the chocolate while the custard is coming up to temperature, or enlist a partner to make one component while you make the other. They won't regret it when it's time to taste the finished product.

PICKLED GREEN STRAWBERRIES

1 cup/250 g Champagne vinegar
⅔ cup/118 g granulated sugar
1½ cups/343 g water
1 pound/454 g large green strawberries, stemmed

Combine the vinegar, sugar, and water in a saucepot, and warm over medium heat, stirring until the sugar is melted. Cool completely. Cover the strawberries with the liquid in a nonreactive airtight container. Fit with a tight lid, and leave in a cool, dry spot for at least 2 weeks.

FERMENTED GREEN STRAWBERRIES

1 pound/454 g green strawberries
1 tablespoon/13.5 g Kosher salt

Wash the berries well in cold water, and pat dry. Purée the berries in a blender with the salt, and transfer to a medium vacuum bag. Seal on high. Leave at room temperature for 3 days or until the bag puffs. Keep the purée in the bag and reserve cold.

DEHYDRATED STRAWBERRIES

20 strawberries, stemmed

Slice the strawberries ¼ inch/6 mm thick, and arrange them on a dehydrating tray that's been misted with nonstick spray. Dehydrate for 12 hours at 125°F or until crisp. Reserve at room temperature.

WHITE CHOCOLATE PUDDING

7 sheets silver gelatin
10 ounces/300 g egg yolk
1 teaspoon/8 g Kosher salt
10 ounces/300 g granulated sugar
2 pounds/1,000 g white chocolate
24 ounces/720 g heavy whipping cream
36 ounces/1,080 g whole milk

Soak the gelatin in cold water until soft. Whip the yolks, salt, and sugar in a stand mixer fitted with the whisk attachment for 5 minutes or until the eggs are pale and fall off the whisk in ribbons.

Cook the white chocolate in a large pot over medium heat, stirring, until it turns a deep caramel color, about 10 minutes.

While the chocolate is caramelizing, bring the cream and milk to a simmer in a medium pot. Slowly temper some of the warm dairy into the eggs on low speed, then pour the egg mixture into the pot. Heat the mixture to 186°F while continuously whisking to make a custard.

Transfer the caramelized white chocolate to a medium bowl. Squeeze out the excess water from the gelatin, and add the gelatin to the chocolate. Slowly add the hot custard. Gently stir the ingredients together with a rubber or silicone spatula, then purée with an immersion blender. Pass the pudding through a chinois into a medium bowl. Set the bowl over a large bowl of ice to chill the pudding. When chilled, transfer to a nonreactive airtight container, and refrigerate until fully set, about 6 hours.

STRAWBERRY PURÉE

2 cups/450 g strawberries, stemmed
3 ounces/85 g granulated sugar
1 teaspoon/3 g malic acid
2 teaspoons/5.5 g agar-agar

Season the berries in a bowl with the sugar and malic acid, cover, and rest at room temperature for 2 hours. Purée the strawberries and their liquid with the agar in a blender. Transfer the purée to a medium pot, and bring to a simmer while continually whisking. Cool completely, and allow to set in the fridge. Purée and reserve in a plastic squeeze bottle at room temperature.

CHOCOLATE CRUMBLE

7 ounces/200 g cocoa powder
7 ounces/200 g granulated sugar
3.5 ounces/100 g Gluten-Free Flour (see page 162)
**   or all-purpose flour**
5 ounces/150 g melted unsalted butter

Preheat the oven to 325°F. Whisk together the cocoa powder, sugar, and flour, and sift. Slowly add the butter until the mixture clumps when squeezed together but still falls apart. Spread the mixture over a sheet tray lined with a silicone baking mat, and bake for 18 to 22 minutes or until dry and firm. Remove the crumble from the oven, allow to cool, and break apart into fine crumbs. Reserve in a cool, dry place.

TO PLATE

2 large strawberries
60 violas

Slice the fresh strawberries and 2 pickled green strawberries into thin rounds, and then cut those rounds into quarters. Spoon 4 ounces/113 g of the pudding into the bottom of a tall bowl (for a playful touch, use a bowl that looks like a flower pot), and generously cover the pudding with the crumble. Add 15 dots of strawberry purée and 7 dots of fermented green strawberry mash. Garnish with 6 pieces each of fresh and pickled green strawberries, 6 pieces of dehydrated strawberry, and 6 violas. Repeat for remaining portions.

COCKTAIL: RUM, JOHNNIE, RUM

Our former beverage director, Jenee Craver, was the president of the Philadelphia chapter of the United States Bartenders' Guild, which organized a Women in Spirits panel for International Women's Day last year. Jenee created this coconut cocktail for the pop-up we hosted next door at In the Valley. She called it a cross between a mai tai and a piña colada, with a backbone of Johnnie Walker Black, an ingredient that's about as common in tropical summer drinks as eggnog. It's interesting how the Scotch works with the overproof rum (we recommend Wray & Nephew) and cream sherry (we recommend Lustau East India Solera); you get the toasted grain up front, the funk of the rum midpalate, and then acid rounding it out and bringing you back for more. About that acid: pineapple juice is the primary agent in this drink. We manipulate its sweetness by blending in citric acid, a cool trick that raises the acidity of the juice to the level of lemon or lime.

MAKES 1 COCKTAIL

PINEAPPLE ACID

15 ounces/440 ml pineapple juice
.2 ounces/5.5 g citric acid

Stir the ingredients together until well combined. Transfer to a plastic squeeze bottle and reserve in the fridge, where it will keep for about 2 weeks.

COCONUT CREAM

8 ounces/237 ml sweetened cream of coconut
3 ounces/89 ml lime juice

Purée the ingredients with an immersion blender until well combined. Transfer to a plastic squeeze bottle and reserve in the fridge, where it will keep for 1 week. Shake before using.

1 ounce/30 ml Scotch
.5 ounce/15 ml overproof rum
.75 ounces/22 ml cream sherry
.75 ounces/22 ml Coconut Cream
.5 ounce/15 ml Pineapple Acid

Pour all the ingredients into a shaker with ice, and quickly shake. Strain into a rocks glass over fresh ice and serve.

PANTRY AND LARDER

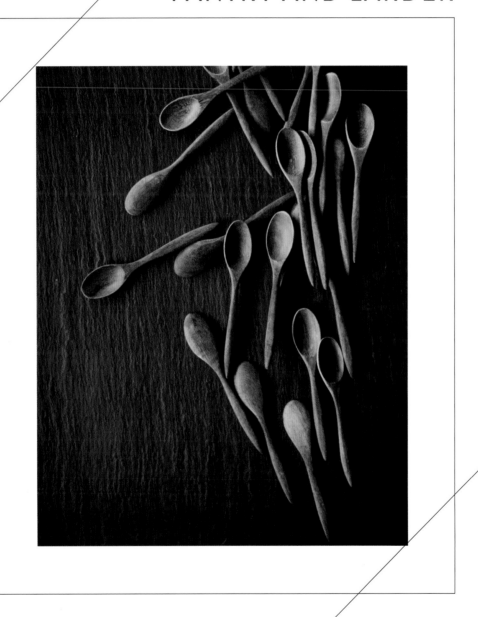

LOBSTER STOCK

MAKES ABOUT 2 QUARTS/2 L

½ white onion
1 pound/454 g cleaned lobster bodies
1 tablespoon/15 g Kosher salt
1 tablespoon/15 g extra-virgin olive oil
2 ounces/60 g sliced carrot
1 leek, halved
1 sprig thyme
2 quarts/2 L water

Preheat the oven to 325°F. Sear the onion cut-side down in a pan over medium heat until the cut side is completely black.

Toss the lobster with the salt and olive oil, and place in a roasting pan. Roast in the oven for 45 minutes, stirring every 10 minutes to prevent sticking. Remove from the oven, and transfer to a pressure cooker with the burned onion, carrot, leek, and thyme. Cover with the water. Cook on high pressure for 35 minutes. Allow the pressure to release naturally. Strain the liquid through two layers of cheesecloth, cool completely, and reserve refrigerated or frozen.

LAMB STOCK

MAKES ABOUT 2 QUARTS/2 L

1 white onion, halved
2 pounds/907 lamb neck bones, cut into 2-inch/
    5-cm pieces
2 tablespoons/30 g Kosher salt
2 tablespoons/30 g extra-virgin olive oil
2 carrots, sliced
1 teaspoon/5 g tomato paste
5 shallots, halved
4 quarts/4 L water

Preheat the oven to 325°F. Sear the onion halves cut-side down in a pan over medium heat until the cut sides are completely black.

Toss the lamb necks with the salt and olive oil, and place in a roasting pan. Roast in the oven until deeply caramelized and cooked through, about 35 minutes. Remove from the oven and transfer to a large pot with the onion, carrot, tomato paste, and shallots. Cover with the water and bring to a simmer, skimming off any fat or impurities as they rise. Reduce slowly for 50 minutes and strain through a chinois. Return the stock to the pot and continue to reduce until the liquid measures about 2 quarts/2 L. Cool completely, and reserve refrigerated or frozen.

ROASTED CHICKEN STOCK

MAKES ABOUT 2 QUARTS/2 L

2 white onions, halved
4 pounds/2 kg chicken bones
1 tablespoon/15 g Kosher salt
1 tablespoon/15 g extra-virgin olive oil
4 shallots, halved
2 sprigs thyme
1 bay leaf
4 quarts/4 L water

Preheat the oven to 325°F. Sear the onion halves cut-side down in a pan over medium heat until the cut sides are completely black.

Toss the chicken bones with the salt and the olive oil, and place in a roasting pan. Roast in the oven until the bones are deeply caramelized and cooked through, about 30 minutes. Remove the bones from the oven, and transfer to a large pot with the onions and the remaining ingredients. Bring to a simmer, skimming off any impurities. Continue to simmer until reduced by a third, and strain through a chinois into a clean pot. Continue to reduce until the liquid measures about 2 quarts/2 L. Cool completely, and reserve refrigerated or frozen.

DUCK JUS

MAKES ABOUT 1 PINT/470 ML

1 pound/454 g duck necks, cut in 2-inch/
   5-cm pieces
¼ cup/60 g grapeseed oil
4 shallots, halved
4 garlic cloves, smashed
½ bulb fennel
1 cup/250 g Burgundy
2 quarts/2 L Roasted Chicken Stock
1 teaspoon/5 g Kosher salt

Sear the duck bones in the oil in a large pot over medium heat. Add the vegetables, and cook until golden, about 8 minutes. Strain off and discard the fat. Deglaze the pan with the wine, and reduce until syrupy. Add the stock, and bring to a simmer. Reduce until the liquid coats the back of a spoon, skimming off any impurities. Strain, and season with the salt. Cool completely, and reserve refrigerated or frozen.

PORK JUS

MAKES ABOUT 1 PINT/470 ML

½ white onion
1 ounce/28 g grapeseed oil
1 pound/454 g pork shoulder cubes
1 tablespoon/15 g Kosher salt, divided
1 leek
3 shallots
1 cup/250 g Chablis
2 quarts/2 L Roasted Chicken Stock
2 ounces/57 g unsalted butter

Sear the onion cut-side down in a pan over medium heat until the cut side is completely black.

Heat the oil in a medium pot over high heat until almost smoking. Toss the pork cubes with half the salt, and cook for 8 minutes until browned all over. Add the onion, leek, and shallots, and cook until caramelized, about 5 minutes. Deglaze the pot with the wine, scraping the bottom to release any bits. Reduce until almost dry. Add the stock, and bring to a simmer, skimming off any impurities. Simmer for 45 minutes. Strain the broth through a chinois into a clean pot, and reduce on high until the liquid coats the back of a spoon. Whisk in the butter and the remaining salt. Cool completely, and reserve refrigerated or frozen.

QUAIL JUS

MAKES ABOUT 1 PINT/470 ML

2 tablespoons/30 g grapeseed oil
1 pound/454 g quail bones and wings
2 shallots, sliced
4 garlic cloves
½ carrot, sliced
1 cup/250 g pinot noir
2 quarts/2 L Roasted Chicken Stock
1 ounce/28 g unsalted butter
1 tablespoon/15 g Kosher salt

Heat the oil in a medium pot over high heat until almost smoking. Add the quail bones and wings, and cook until lightly browned. Add the vegetables, and cook until caramelized, about 5 minutes. Deglaze the pot with the wine, and reduce until almost dry. Add the stock, and bring to a simmer, skimming off any impurities. Simmer for 30 minutes. Strain through a chinois into a clean pot, and reduce on high until the liquid coats the back of a spoon. Whisk in the butter and salt. Cool completely, and reserve refrigerated or frozen.

BRINES, PICKLES, AND VINEGARS

DUCK BRINE

MAKES 1 QUART/1 L

1 quart/1 L water
1.6 ounces/45.4 g Kosher salt

Bring the water and salt to a simmer in a large pot, stirring to dissolve the salt. Cool completely, and reserve refrigerated or frozen.

MEAT BRINE

MAKES ABOUT 2 QUARTS/2 L

1 cup/228 g Kosher salt
½ cup/114 g packed light brown sugar
1 tablespoon/10 g black peppercorns
⅛ cup/28 g pink salt
1 teaspoon/5 g yellow mustard seeds
8 allspice berries
8 whole cloves
2 bay leaves
1 cinnamon stick
39 ounces/1,150 g water
32 ounces/1,000 g ice

Combine all ingredients except the ice in a large pot, and bring to a boil, stirring to dissolve the salts and sugar. Remove the pot from the heat and add the ice, stirring until the liquid is completely chilled. Transfer to plastic quart containers, and reserve refrigerated or frozen. Keeps for 2 weeks.

SWEET PICKLE BRINE

MAKES 2 QUARTS/2 L

20 ounces/600 g Champagne vinegar
10.4 ounces/300 g granulated sugar
4 teaspoons/20 g Kosher salt
1 quart/1 L water

Combine all the ingredients in a large pot and bring to a boil, stirring to dissolve the sugar and salt. Cool completely, transfer to plastic quart containers, and reserve refrigerated or frozen.

PICKLED ELDERBERRIES

10 ounces/300 g red wine vinegar
5.3 ounces/150 g granulated sugar
16 ounces/.5 L water
1 pound/456 g stemmed elderberries

Bring the vinegar, sugar, and water to simmer, stirring to dissolve the sugar. Cool completely. Place the berries in a large vacuum bag, and pour the cooled liquid over them. Seal on medium. Refrigerate for 2 weeks. Keeps for 1 year.

PICKLED BABY CORN

20 ears baby corn in the husk
2 cups/470 g Sweet Pickle Brine

Preheat the oven to 325°F. Remove the husks from the baby corn. Discard half the husks, and toast the remaining husks until lightly golden, about 10 minutes.

Warm the brine. Add the husks, cover, remove from the heat, and steep for 30 minutes. Place the corn in a medium vacuum bag. Strain the brine through a fine sieve, and add it to the bag. Seal on high, and set aside for at least 4 days in the fridge.

ELDERBERRY VINEGAR

1 cinnamon stick
2 cups/45 g dried elderberries
2 quarts/2,000 g Champagne vinegar
3 tablespoons/35 g granulated sugar
½ cup/100 g water

Char the cinnamon stick all over with a crème brûlée torch, and place it in a nonreactive container. Purée the remaining ingredients in a blender until smooth, and add to the container with the cinnamon. Cover with cheesecloth, and leave in a cool, dry place for 2 weeks. Strain the vinegar into a clean bottle, and reserve in the refrigerator for up to 3 months.

RHUBARB VINEGAR

5 pounds/2.3 kg rhubarb
2 quarts/2,000 g white balsamic vinegar
½ cup/100 g granulated sugar
4 cardamom pods

Peel the rhubarb, reserving the peels for this recipe and the fruit for a future use. Dehydrate the peels at 145°F for 6 hours. Purée in a blender with the vinegar and sugar. Place the purée in a nonreactive container, and add the cardamom. Cover with cheesecloth, and leave in a cool, dry place for 2 weeks. Strain the vinegar into a clean bottle and reserve.

FERMENTED AND DRIED INGREDIENTS

On Fermentation

I went to the 2018 MAD conference in Copenhagen last summer, and David Zilber, the chef in charge of Noma's fermentation program, described the technique perfectly. "Fermentation is just another style of cooking," he said. "It just takes a little longer." It's a huge part of what we do at Laurel and probably our favorite "cooking" method. Ferments take time to mature—a week, a month, a year—but you can't develop that truly special, complex umami any other way.

Many of the recipes in this book call for fermented ingredients. While traditional methods call for fermenting foodstuffs in ceramic crocks and glass jars, we often prefer vacuum bags. They save space, but they also give us a visual cue for when fermentation begins. When foods ferment, they release gas. In a vacuum-sealed environment, that gas has nowhere to go, so the bag puffs. A puffed bag is like the ding that lets you know your oven is preheated; it means things are ready to really start cooking. The majority of the ferments in this book hang out for one to two weeks. The time is based on how far we want to take the fermented flavor: the longer you go, the stronger the flavor. We tell you to pull the ingredient when we think the taste is right for the dish.

That said, every ingredient is different. No batch of fermented sunchokes will be exactly the same because not every sunchoke has the same water content (and the water is what's actually fermenting). The temperature and humidity in the location where you're doing the fermenting can also affect the process. So watch for the puff, and you'll know you're on the right track. That's first.

Second, you have to taste. You can roast a chicken at 325°F for forty-five minutes, but you still need to physically touch it and feel it and understand it to know when it's done. Fermentation, same thing. You can follow all the guidelines we've laid out in this book, but the best way to know when a ferment is ready is to touch (always with clean hands) and taste and build up that knowledge bank. The more you do it, the better you get. A fermented food should taste salty and pleasantly funky and delicious. If it tastes . . . *wrong*, you'll know it. Spoilage can occur if the seal fails on a bag or if some rogue element was introduced into the fermentation environment. The chance that you'll eat it by accident is pretty unlikely. There's no confusing a fermented food and a rotten one. The human body has evolved to recognize the difference.

FERMENTED CROSNES

1 pound/454 g crosnes
.5 ounce/14 g Kosher salt

Toss the crosnes with the salt. Transfer to a medium vacuum bag, seal on high, and reserve in a cool, dry place for 1 week; the bag may puff slightly. Reserve cold.

FERMENTED DAYLILIES

1 pound/454 g daylily roots
1 tablespoon/15 g salt

Combine the ingredients in a large vacuum bag, seal on high, and leave at room temperature for 2 weeks or until the bag puffs. Reserve cold.

BLACK SHALLOTS

2 shallots, unpeeled

Rinse and peel the shallots, leaving the root intact. Place the shallots in a nonreactive container, and wrap the container in plastic wrap several times to make it airtight. Place the container in a dehydrator set at 120°F for 2 weeks or until the shallots change color to a deep black-brown. Remove from the dehydrator, and reserve cold until ready to use. Keeps 2 weeks.

FERMENTED SCALLION POWDER

3 bunches scallions
Kosher salt

Roughly chop the green scallion tops, reserving anything that is white for another purpose. Weigh the scallion tops, and add 3 percent of the scallions' weight in salt. Mix well, transfer to a large vacuum bag, and seal on high. Leave at room temperature for 1 week; the bag may puff slightly. Remove from the bag, and strain off any liquid.

Dehydrate the scallion tops for 4 days at 125°F. Grind the dehydrated scallions in a spice grinder, and reserve in a mesh-top shaker.

SOCHAN POWDER

1 pound/454 sochan leaves
.5 ounce/13.5 g Kosher salt

Season the sochan with the salt, and place it in a large vacuum bag. Seal on high, and leave it in a cool, dry place for 1 week; the bag may puff slightly. Open bag and drain off any liquid.

Set a dehydrator to 95°F. Lay the leaves on the tray, and dehydrate for 12 hours or until completely dry. Powder the dried sochan in a spice mill. Reserve at room temperature in a mesh-top shaker.

FERMENTED BLACK TRUMPET POWDER

8 ounces/227 g black trumpet mushrooms
¼ ounce/7 g Kosher salt

Season the mushrooms with the salt, and transfer to a large vacuum bag. Seal on high, and leave at room temperature for 2 weeks or until the bag puffs.

Strain the mushrooms, and dehydrate them for 24 hours at 140°F. Grind the dehydrated mushrooms in a spice grinder. Reserve in a mesh-top shaker.

FERMENTED GARLIC SCAPES

1 pound/454 g garlic scapes
½ ounce/14.4 g Kosher salt

Pulse the scapes and salt into a fine paste in a food processor. Transfer the mixture to a large vacuum bag, seal on high, and leave in a cool, dry place for 1 week. Strain out the mixture, discarding the liquid and reserving the pulp. Reserve cold.

BLACK LIME POWDER

1 lime, halved

Preheat the oven to 425°F. Places the lime halves cut-side up directly on oven's the center rack, with a sheet pan placed on the rack directly below. Cook for about 4 hours or until the lime halves are completely black throughout. Cool completely. Powder the limes in a spice grinder, and reserve in a mesh-top shaker.

GLUTEN-FREE FLOUR

MAKES 4½ POUNDS/2 KG

2.2 pounds/1,000 g brown rice flour
1.8 pounds/800 g white rice flour
7 ounces/200 g tapioca flour
1 ounce/26 g xanthan gum

Whisk all the ingredients together. Transfer to a non-reactive container, and store in a cool, dry place.

BITTER GREENS PURÉE

MAKES ABOUT 1 CUP/220 G

2 quarts/2 L water
Kosher salt
½ bunch black kale
½ bunch collard greens
½ teaspoon/1 g Ultra-Tex 8

Bring the water to a boil, and season it heavily with salt. Strip the kale and the collards from their stems. Blanch the greens for 4 minutes; remove them from the boiling water and shock them in a bowl of ice water. Remove the greens from the ice water, lay them out on a dish towel, roll the towel up, and squeeze out the excess water. Blend the greens in a blender, adding ice water if necessary to achieve a thick, sturdy consistency; the purée should hold its shape when scooped and set on a plate. Add the Ultra-Tex 8, and purée. Transfer to a plastic squeeze bottle and reserve cold. Keeps 1 week.

CHIVE OIL

MAKES ABOUT 3 OUNCES/85 G

1 bunch chives
4 ounces/115 g grapeseed oil
1 teaspoon/5 g Kosher salt

Purée all the ingredients together, and transfer to a medium pot. Bring to a simmer, constantly stirring with a rubber spatula, until the oil separates from the solids. Strain through a chinois into a small bowl. Discard the solids. Set the bowl over a medium bowl filled with ice, stirring the oil to chill it. Transfer the oil to a plastic squeeze bottle, and reserve cold. Keeps 1 week.

KALE OIL

MAKES ABOUT 2 OUNCES/50 G

2 bunches black kale
¼ cup/58 g grapeseed oil
½ teaspoon/2.5 g Kosher salt

Purée the kale and the oil in a blender until combined. Pour the mixture into a medium pot, and bring to a simmer, constantly stirring with a spatula. Cook until the solids and oil break, about 3 minutes. Strain through a chinois into a bowl set into a larger bowl of ice. Stir the oil to chill it. Transfer the oil to a plastic squeeze bottle and reserve cold. Keeps 1 week.

MEYER LEMON PURÉE

MAKES ABOUT 16 OUNCES/454 G

10 Meyer lemons
¼ cup/58 g grapeseed oil
1 tablespoon/10 g granulated sugar

Using a vegetable peeler, remove the rind from the lemons, being sure to not leave any pith attached to the rinds. Juice the lemons, strain out any seeds, and reserve the juice in a nonreactive airtight container.

Place the rinds in a medium pot, cover with cold water, and bring to a boil. Strain out the rinds, place them back in the pot, cover again in cold water and bring to a boil. Repeat this process a total of 10 times. After the final strain, place the rinds in a blender. Purée with the oil, sugar, and enough lemon juice to make the purée slightly acidic, about 2 ounces/59 g. Strain the mixture through a chinois into a plastic squeeze bottle and reserve cold. Keeps 1 week.

HERB PURÉE

MAKES ABOUT 1 CUP/220 G

2 quarts/2 L water
2 cups/450 g Kosher salt
3 ounces/85 g flat-leaf parsley leaves
3 ounces/85 g chervil leaves
3 ounces/85 g tarragon leaves
1 bunch chives
1 tablespoon/6 g Ultra-Tex 8
1 tablespoon/15 g extra-virgin olive oil

Bring a large pot of water to boil, and season with the salt. Blanch all the herbs for 4 minutes, and immediately shock in ice water. Purée the herbs in a blender until smooth. Add the Ultra-Tex and continue to purée. Pass through a chinois. Fold in the olive oil, and adjust the salt as needed. Reserve cold in a plastic squeeze bottle. Keeps 1 week.

GLOSSARY OF PLANTS AND PRODUCE

FARMED

Anise hyssop: A mint-family herb with a bright anise flavor and perfume.

Bachelor's button: Also known as blue cornflower, a bud with the mild flavor of corn silk.

Borage: A plant with a vegetal oyster-cucumber flavor; the leaves and star-shaped, periwinkle-blue flowers are both edible.

Buddha's hand: A citrus we love for its rind, which smells like a lemon Jolly Rancher. It grows upside-down and looks like a hand full of fingers.

Calamansi: An aggressive citrus that tastes like a cross between yuzu and kumquat, with bitter orange overtones.

Cardamom leaf: The long, slender, very fragrant leaf of the cardamom plant.

Celtuce: A root that tastes strongly of romaine.

Chrysanthemum sprouts: Also known as shungiku, the small sprouts of the chrysanthemum plant.

Crosne: Also known as Japanese artichoke, a root vegetable with pale, delicate skin that lends well to pickling and fermenting.

Green coriander: The unripe buds of coriander that taste like a refreshing cross between coriander seeds and cilantro.

Lovage: An herb with an intense celery-parsley flavor.

Makrut lime: A citrus native to Asia with a pebbled rind, bitter juice, and highly aromatic leaves. The leaves are the component most commonly called for in recipes and can be used fresh or dried.

Salsify flowers: The flowering part of the salsify plant; they taste strongly of artichoke.

Sochan: Also known as green-headed coneflower, a native North American plant with a flavor similar to that of lovage.

Sudachi: A Japanese lime similar to yuzu.

FORAGED

Black locust flowers: A true sign of spring, these flowers taste like the sweetest of spring peas.

Daylilies: Roots and shoots of an edible lily with a light oniony flavor.

Ground ivy: Tastes like a cross between oregano and sage, with a meaty scent that pairs well with lamb.

Hercules' club: Young shoots, one- to seven-inches in length, with a subtle artichoke flavor; also known as taranome.

Knotweed: An invasive spring plant with a flavor similar to that of rhubarb (which makes a good substitute).

Salty Fingers: A crunchy, salty succulent harvested from coastal regions; substitute sea beans.

Toothwort: A mustard-family root with a mild horseradish flavor.

Violas: Small purple and yellow violets with a subtle violet flavor.

ACKNOWLEDGMENTS

FROM NICK

When I need strength, clarity, understanding, and love I look to my wife, Kristen. Thank you, Kris, for everything you have done for me and our family. Your calm kindness is infectious and you've been my inspiration countless times. I find myself to be unbelievably lucky you chose me to be your partner.

I've had the opportunity to work with hundreds of chefs and cooks through my years, and Eddie Konrad is easily the most talented human I've cooked beside. Eddie is tasked with running day-to-day operations at Laurel and has taken the restaurant to new heights. I'm lucky to call him a friend. Eddie, I'm so very excited to see where your career takes you.

My dear friend and business partner, Jonathan Cohen, blindly believed in me and has supported me, my family, and the restaurant from the very beginning. Always encouraging. Always defending. Always resolute. Thank you to my current and former staff at Laurel and In the Valley, including Jane Fryer, our wonderful manager, Jason Chavenson, my right-hand-man during the photo shoots for this book, and Jenee Carver, who developed the cocktail recipes.

FROM ADAM

Charlotte, you are my biggest cheerleader. When I said I wanted to get into writing cookbooks and stressed about how to do so, you told me, "if others can do it, so can you." You were right, I did, and I love you. Thank you to my parents, especially my mom, who signed me up (and made me attend, despite protests) a pre-college writing program at Philadelphia magazine. We published a teen mag in which I wrote stories about high school bookies and where to go for spring break. I owe a great deal to editors who helped open doors for me as a young writer, among them April White, Vicki Glembocki, Tammy Paolino, Joy Manning, Francis Lam, and Greg Emmanuel. Whether they know it or not, cookbook authors Cheryl Alters-Jamison and the late Bill Jamison are huge inspirations.

FROM BOTH OF US

Our agent, Clare Pelino, has been with this project from day one. Thanks, Clare, for you guidance and support in what is hopefully the first of many. To our photographer, Neal Santos, we value your talent and friendship. The last time your photos and our words and food intersected was the *City Paper* review of Rittenhouse Tavern in 2012—we've all come a long way since then. Your gorgeous photography brought this book to life, and your easygoing spirit made the jam-packed shoots a pleasure. Thank you to the team at Running Press: designer Joshua McDonnell, editor Kristen Green Wiewora, publisher Kristin Kiser, project editor Cisca Schreefel, and copyeditor Kelley Blewster. We can't wait to do this again.

INDEX

Note: Page references in *italics* indicate photographs.

C

Calamansi

    about, 165

    Broth, 61

Caramel

    Black Walnut Powder, 40

    Caramel-Coffee Cream, 39

Cardamom leaf, about, 165

Caviar, Paddlefish, Vodka Cream, Salsify Ice Cream, *124*, 136–137

Celery Root

    Glazed, 77–78

    Reduction, 77

Celtuce, about, 165

Chamomile and White Peach Nage, 101

Champagne Chicken Broth, 104

Cheese

    Gnocchi, 71

Cherry(ies)

    Glaze, 144

    Grilled Quail, Black Garlic Scape, *128*, 144–145

Chicken

    Champagne Broth, 104

    Jus, 74

    Roasted, Stock, 156

Chicory Crumble, 35

Chive Oil, 163

Chocolate Crumble, 151

Chrysanthemum sprouts, 165

Citric acid, xxxiv

Citrus juices, xxxv

Clams

    Truffle Custard, 63

Cocktails

    A Bird Named Barb, *95*, 118

    Drunken Farmer, *11*, 42

    The Kali, *55*, 84

    Rum, Johnnie, Rum, *131*, 152

Coconut Cream, 152

Coffee-Caramel Cream, 39

Consommé, Apple Yuzu, 12

Cordial, Fennel, 42

Coriander, Green

    about, 165

    Pickled, 134

Corn

    Baby, Pickled, 159

    Creamed-Corn, Mousse, 19

Crab

    Broth, 140

    Soft-Shell, Custard, 141

Cream

    Caramel-Coffee, 39

    Oyster, 103

    Vodka, 137

Cremodan 30, xxxiv

Crosne(s)

    about, 165

    Fermented, 161

Crumbles

    Chicory, 35

    Chocolate, 151

Curd, Yuzu, 80

Custards

    Soft-Shell Crab, 141

    Truffle, 63

D

Dashi and Mackerel, 29

Daylily(ies)

    about, 166

    Fermented, 161

    Kimchi, 111

    Shoots, Dried Beef Heart, *86*, 98

Dehydrator, xxxviii

Desserts

    Honeysuckle-Poached Rhubarb, Ice Cream, Knotweed Jam, Lovage Granite, *94*, 116–117

    Roasted Apple, Caramel-Coffee Cream, Black Walnut, Apple Wine, *10*, 38–41

    White Chocolate Pudding, Cocoa Crumble, Strawberries, *130*, 148–151

    Yuzu Curd, Black Sesame, Torched Malt Crisp, *54*, 80–81

Drunken Farmer, *11*, 42

Duck

    Breast, Cured, 35

    Breasts, 37

    Brine, 158

    Jus, 156

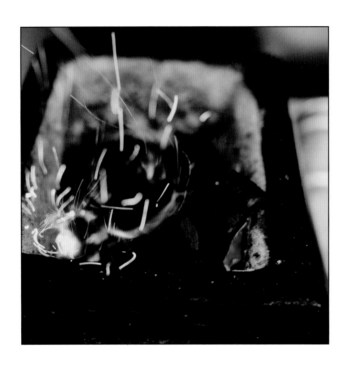

S

W

Walnut, Black, Caramel Powder, 40

Watercress

    Oil, 32

    Purée, 32

Whey Onions, 74

Whipped Apple, 13

White Chocolate Pudding, 149

White soy sauce, xxxv

Winter menu

    Black Trumpet Mushroom–Stuffed Dover Sole, Chicken Jus, Whey Onions, *52*, 72–75

    Bourbon-Glazed Grilled Lobster, Crunchy Grains, Apple Blossoms, *50*, 66–69

    Cocktail: The Kali, *55*, 84

    Fresh Ricotta Gnocchi, Black Truffle, Toasted Sourdough, *51*, 70–71

    Frozen Beet, Sumac, Pomegranate, *46*, 56–57

    Hay-Cured Squab en Vessie, *53*, 76–78

    Kasu-Cured Fluke, Citrus, Olive Oil, *47*, 60–61

    Pan-Roasted Halibut Cheek, White Asparagus, Quince Confit, *49*, 64–65

    Warm Truffle Custard, Surf Clam, Makrut Lime, *48*, 62–63

    Yuzu Curd, Black Sesame, Torched Malt Crisp, *54*, 80–81

X

Xanthan gum, xxxv

Y

Yuzu

    about, xxxv

    Apple Consommé, 12

    Apple Gelée, 12

    Curd, 80

Z

Zucchini, Maine Mussels, Saffron, *125*, 138–139